"On the second day of school I realised that no one knew what they were doing and I would have to make my own way."

A Curious & Inelegant Childhood

A Curious & Inelegant Childhood is a delightful story that will entertain any reader. *MANIC READERS.*

LINDA RUTH BROOKS

GUM TREE press

Copyright: Linda Ruth Brooks © 2010

Formerly *An Australian Childhood*

All rights reserved. This book is copyright protected. Apart from any fair dealings for the purpose of private study, criticism, research or review as permitted under the *Copyright Act (Australia)*, no part may be reproduced by any process without written permission. Enquiries should be addressed to the copyright owner.

 A copy of this book can be found in the National Library of Australia, Canberra

Cover & interior design: *LRB Publishing Services*
lindaruthbrooks@bigpond.com
Photographs: author's own
Watercolour artwork © Linda Brooks

ISBN: 978-1-7642121-3-7; 978-0-6455650-8-9
ISBN: 978-0646-52603-4

Literary nonfiction/humour/memoir
This book, and others by Linda Ruth Brooks, may be purchased through amazon.com, Booktopia & online bookstores..

Author

Linda Brooks lives in Adelaide. She writes nonfiction, poetry, fiction and short stories. She has published and illustrated children's books.

Linda completed a BA Hons in Creative Writing from Southern Cross University (2019). She gained a publisher for her childhood memoir *A Curious & Inelegant Childhood*. She has written a nonfiction book on living with Asperger's Syndrome (autism spectrum) *I'm not broken, I'm just different* and the children's book *Callan the Chameleon* with contributions from Professor Tony Attwood.

Published in anthologies: *Coastlines 5, 6, 7 & 8* by Southern Cross University; *Wood, Bricks & Stone*, Catchfire Press; *Grieve*, Newcastle Writers Centre; *Third Wednesday Poets*; *Seeking the Sun*, Central Coast Poets; *Times Past* Stringybark Press and *Longing for Solitude*.

Awards: Rebecca Coyle Scholarship for Hons; first prize for Legacy University Level Creative Writing Award; first prize in the Gabe Reynaud Creative Writing Award and the Mater Misericordiae Grieve Writing Award.

A registered nurse and advocate for disability in a previous life, Linda has a rich background in listening to the stories of others, never shying away from the darker, gritty tales. And yet, humour is never far away. Linda enjoys hearing from her readers:

lindaruthbrooks@bigpond.com

Author titles

Nonfiction:
I'm not broken, I'm just different
(on Asperger's with Professor Tony Attwood)
A Curious and Inelegant Childhood

Adult fiction:
Behind Whispering Hands
Butterfly Pinning
The Unprize
A broken hallelujah
Scarlett doesn't live here anymore
Under the Bracken Fern

Children's books:
A Tabby Never Forgets
Callan the Chameleon (Asperger's Syndrome)
Dusty Bunny's Very Important Job
Izzy & Pudding the Cat
I want a monkey!
Madam Iris Bigglesworth
The Banyula Tales - 6 stories
Who Stole Christmas?

Publisher of the anthologies:
We are Australian'
The Great Australian Shed
Waltzing Matilda

Contents

Introduction	1
I arrive on this planet	3
Escape while you can!	8
A Royal fuss	13
An ancestral brush with fame	16
Dad and me	20
I don't need another hero	24
Of Danger and Dunnies	30
I want to cuddle a Koala	34
Wanna go out?	40
Life on the creek	43
Sunday School Blues	47
I Came, I Saw, I Failed	53
The boy who ran	59
The haunted house at 49	62
It Takes a Village to Raise a Child	67
I remember . . .	71
My first bully	75
The Great Australian Shed	77
'I'm going to teach you jolly kids manners!'	81
The Great Escape	87
Hospital nightmare	90
Cobalt princess	94
'Is it too much for a person to ask?'	98
A dangerous time	103
Dad's apprentice	107
Cuz Buddy	116

My Friend Bettina	120
Sharing a secret	124
Puberty panic	131
No pain, no gain	135
Kamikaze Kitty	138
A fine romance	142
'Don't leave your manners at home.'	147
Toe to Toe	150
Christmas Rescued	152
What could possibly go wrong?	157
The secret life of my father	163
They shot my Daddy with a gun!	168
'Who the blazes...'	173
A banana	178
I am trouble	181
Child Whisperer	190
A Sporting Chance	193
The fettler	196
Shingle Splitters Summers	200
Freedom comes	203
A new fish bowl	207
First job	215
Accidental feminist & part-time tyrant	218
The love virus	220
Mr Sox dies and I want to grow up	223
Country 'Snobs'	227
Don't kiss me, I like it!	232
Romance grows up and so do I	237

'We're breaking out!'	247
The patience of the Saints	253
Mum's Get Rich Schemes	258
School ends; a new horizon beckons	263
Goodbye lunch with Mum	267
À bientôt, mes amis	272
Farewell to home	277
Commies, feminism and ignorance	280
Acknowledgements	284

*Dedicated to the engineer and the stenographer,
Max and Elsie Brooks, who decided to celebrate
their love by making me, and to my brother Peter,
who thinks the book is about him.*

Introduction

I was born in the early summer of 1954 to a meticulous stenographer who saw life in rigid lines. When she became a parent, she was shocked to find that children were not as easy to manage as typewriters and adding machines. This confused her all her life. Why were we not like numbers that added up to predictable outcomes?

She said, 'I call a spade a spade'—while holding a shovel and, 'I'm a plain Jane, you can't make a silk purse out of a sow's ear'. She didn't say, 'I love you,' very often but she said, 'Mothers feel every pain their child feels. You will know this when you have children.'

My father was a creative engineer with undeniable Irish lineage, a natural talent for music and a wicked sense of humour hidden by a shyness that meant few knew the real man. Disinterested in the past, he ignored the family tree until he found that his side of the family had aristocratic ancestry and Mum's had convicts.

Thereafter he called himself a thoroughbred, with a childlike glint of mischief in his eye, goading Mum to say, 'At least we know a day's work when we see it.'

Dad was a gentle soul who was a peacemaker. People would use his time and talents and then give little in return. Mum wanted to 'sort them out' but Dad would gently say,

'We're told to turn the other cheek, Else.'

'You've only got two cheeks, Max,' was Mum's pithy reply.

Dad kept his silence through life—gracious to all. Mum, on the other hand left nothing unsaid; only the dead missed her meaning.

I arrive on this planet

I was born late according to the apparently infallible due date that the doctor had calculated would be my time of arrival. This practice I continued for much of my life and was often commented on by my mother, who was prone to say, 'Linda would be late for her own funeral.'

Although a little bleary because of a generous application of 'the mask', which delivered the pain relief gas, nitrous oxide mixed with oxygen, she heard the Doctor say, 'It's a girl and she is perfect.' This particular fact was often disputed by my mother with some enthusiasm.

The Doctor applied a swift slap to my bum, as was the custom of the day, in order to make me breathe.

My mother continued this practice enthusiastically for the next twelve years of my life, in order to stop me from breathing—so that she would not have to listen to the constant torrent of words that came from my unruly mouth. 'That girl has been infected with a gramophone needle,' she would say—referring to the technical apparatus of the era that supplied you with noise all day long. Of course, the gramophone supplied music and I fell quite short of any musical talent, but Mum felt this was a fitting description of my garrulous nature.

I was joyful and spontaneous because the world I had arrived in was a world of wonder. I was filled with both fascination and enchantment with each new adventure and each new person who entered my world. This made little sense to my mother.

My mother was 36 and her short wavy brown hair had not a whisper of grey. With my birth three and a half years after my brother's arrival she had produced a pigeon pair, which meant one of each sex. She was elated at her success in this regard. She was even more proud that she had first produced a son and then a daughter. So, in the true English style that she upheld, she had produced an heir and then a daughter.

This achievement gave her no end of pride and no-one could ever convince her that this arrangement had nothing to do with her, but was controlled by nature. The fact that my parents were actually quite poor and didn't even own a car—which effectively meant there was no dynasty for the heir, did not detract from my mother's pride in the marvellous order of the arrival of her children.

Perhaps she thought the dynasty would arrive one day. Or perhaps having been raised with the severe and relentless work ethic of the country folk of the 1930's, she believed that good hard work would supply her with the eventual justified reward of prosperity.

Even though reality did not supply her very much in the way of material goods, she continued to pretend that the abundant life was just around the corner. Her life was a constant struggle. This belief caused her to overdo everything. If she did not achieve prosperity, it would not be because she did not deserve it, and to earn it she must apply every thought and muscle to physical work of some kind. This made little sense to me.

Our home reflected this in every nook and cranny. The copious gardens that edged every side of the house were designed to require the kind of attention that could have only been supplied by several gardeners, but my mother was up to the challenge. She applied the kind of drive and physical effort that made any television gardening renovation program look like kindergarten.

She was an unstoppable force of nature—a one woman army. Every inch of the garden was crammed with some kind of plant life, creating a cacophony of smells rather than a fragrant ambience. In tune with her workaholic ethic, she planted annuals as well as perennials and chose the most difficult plants to grow. She made determined efforts to obtain plants that were not suited to the climate or conditions of our area and believed that they would prosper by the sheer force of her considerable will.

They didn't. Even though she placed plastic bags nightly over the tropical plants all through winter to protect them from the killing frosts, they never flowered, although they survived, stunted and mute.

She especially loved frangipanis and even though she was singularly unsuccessful with them, she never allowed herself to give up. One day she would prevail.

We lived in a house typical of those in our street, unlike other areas in our town—where old weatherboard houses with disreputable exteriors sat side by side with brick and tile double-storey masterpieces. Our house was a big square white weatherboard. It was not permitted to fade like those of our neighbours. It wouldn't have dared.

However, all of her days in this house, my mother was offended by weatherboard. The constant thought of its upkeep hung over her head. She put her considerable energy into pressuring my father to 'do the place up'.

I found this 'doing up' process very confusing as a child, because it didn't appear to me to be a case of actually improving anything, but merely rearranging. This was also the time of my mother's burgeoning love affair with anything garishly orange or luridly lime green.

When I was about five, the master bedroom became the kitchen, and with the extraordinary logic known only to my mother, this was achieved by actually using the same kitchen cupboards and appliances.

My thoughts on the matter were given. It was swiftly enforced on me that my opinion had not been sought and was indeed not required. I was a child. What would I know of the world of 'grownups'?

If the twinkle in my father's eye betrayed his consensus with me, it was not spoken out loud. He quite justly feared he would receive precisely the same advice I'd been given. Apparently we were both children. He was just a more useful and pliable child than me.

The laundry, a room at the back of the house, contained a huge copper tub with a firebox under it to heat water for washing. The clothes were agitated with a large stick, 'the copper stick', not unlike a thick broomstick, worked by my mother's strong back and arms. This arrangement had an eerie resemblance to a witch's cauldron.

Dad shifted the copper tub to the shed and installed a shower cubicle in its place. Then the room was referred to as the bathroom. With the arrival of our new automatic washing machine it became the laundry again. The room still contained all the bathroom essentials so I was at a loss to know what to call it, as we already had another bathroom—that had once been a large broom closet.

Escape while you can!

Our Uncle Gordon was not just an uncle but a destination. In the late 1950's he lived with his wife Alice in the same street as us. It was a typical small, country-town dirt road with wide gravel edges. It was a dead end street and my family lived at the dead end—the last house at the top end of the street.

Uncle Gordon and Auntie Alice lived about 12 houses down on the other side of the road. Because the houses were on large blocks this was about half a mile. They didn't have any children but were excessively fond of small dogs, orchids and my brother, Peter and me. This affection suited us children greatly. We called Uncle Gordon, 'Gorgie', and were a little more formal with Auntie Alice. Due to their welcoming warmth and Auntie Alice's cake making ability, my brother Peter and I experienced strong desires to go and visit them—often.

I adored my older brother and called him Pee Pee Boy. Everywhere Pee Pee Boy went I wanted to go. Being five years old, he was light years faster than me. This gave him a decided advantage in making spontaneous visits to Gorgie's house. I wanted to go and I was not subtle in my requests.

'Can I go to Gorgie's place, pwease Mum, Can I? Can I?' I lisped as I hopped from one foot to the other. 'I wuv Gorgie, Mum. I wuv Auntie Alice too. She makes orange cake, Mum. She makes orange cake every day, Mum.'

'Don't nag, Linda,' Mum said, sighing heavily.

'Not nagging, Mum, dust asking, can I?'

'No! You can't go! You're too little to go on your own.'

'Then you take me Mum, pwease!' I pulled on her apron, as she pegged out the washing, just in case this would persuade her.

'Don't yank at me! You're not going! I'm not going! Nobody's going to Uncle Gordon's!'

'Pee Pee Boy is! He's nilly dere!'

'Oh damn, Max'll kill me!' she yelped as she looked down the dusty road, to see Peter peddling his bright red car like greased lightning to Gorgie's.

'Max! That boy's escaped again! Kid's a blooming Houdini,' she called to my father, who wandered out of the shed wiping black grease from his hands.

'Not again! How do you let this happen, Else? Kid's only five. Why don't you keep an eye on him?'

'You try keeping an eye on him, Max. The blooming kid's gone like the shot out of a gun.'

'Can't be that fast, Else,' Dad said calmly until he realised there was a car coming up the quiet street, and then he bolted after Peter.

'It's not my fault!' Mum yelled. 'You made the damn car.'

It was true. To the envy of the neighbourhood we owned marvellous things made by Dad no one else could afford. He had crafted the little car meticulously, painting it fire engine red. Peter was seldom out of it. With me on the bonnet he gave me guided tours of our backyard. Whatever he told me to do, I did instantly, without question—much to Mum's dismay.

Dad arrived back home carrying the pedal car with Peter trundling beside him. Because it was some distance to Gorgie's, Peter had had time for the social niceties and was smiling happily with his face stuffed full of Auntie Alice's latest cake. It was obviously worth the effort.

'Why'd you let him have cake?' Mum remonstrated.

'Could hardly make the kid spit it out, Else,' Dad responded rationally.

The look on Mum's face said she might have given it a try, but then again, maybe not. Mum couldn't resist Auntie Alice's cakes either. They were the stuff of legend. And no matter how tough Mum was, she couldn't abide her children going without food. When other mothers told her they had sent their children to bed without tea, Mum was gobsmacked.

'Good grief, I could never do that. There are enough countries where kids are starving.' The parents on the receiving end of this remark stopped in their tracks.

Mum and Dad scratched their heads over a suitable punishment for Peter, preferably one that would curtail his spontaneous adventures. While they were discussing this, Peter gave me several tours of the backyard. They usually decided to take the car off him. Never one to throw a tantrum or complain Peter accepted the decision with calm resignation, knowing Dad wasn't very creative about hiding the car and he'd find it quicker than Dad could hide it. Dad was a busy man, but Peter had nothing better to do than keep track of his car.

Not much later, it would start all over again.

'Max!'

'What now Else? Can't a man put a tyre on a car without a disaster?'

'Kid's gone again. Can't see him for dust.'

When Dad wasn't there Mum would become very anxious about these escape routines. We lived near the bush and when Peter wasn't heading to Gorgie's for cake and conversation, he was climbing through the barbed wire fence, heading to the thick bush with the adventurous passion of explorers Burke and Wills. While Mum could manage a bit of a gallop after him down the dusty road, she could not get through the barbed wire fence. I can picture her desperately trying to wrap both apron and skirt between her legs while trying to hold both the top and bottom wires, inevitably getting caught in the barbs and muttering, 'Damn!'

When Mum told me the story later, she said that when she returned from rescuing Peter from escaping under the fence, she found that I had tipped all her pegs out and was lining them up in colourful rainbows. Another tantrum would begin, as she muttered, 'How is a person expected to get anything done around here?'

Dad was getting a bit more tense and terse with each occasion. One day he came home to find Mum hanging out the washing peacefully with me at her feet. Then he spied Peter tied to the clothesline.

'Oh, for crying out loud Else! Did you have to go that far? Kid's not an animal!'

'No, he's a blooming comet!' She sighed. 'Well, if you don't like it, you think of something better,' Mum wasn't the least intimidated by Dad's shocked tone. 'At least it kept him in the yard.'

Dad was speechless, so Mum decided on a different approach. 'Anyway, I saw a red belly black snake near the fence this morning.'

A Royal fuss

In 1954 the Queen visited Australia. She was to be driven through the streets of Newcastle and my mother was determined not to miss this piece of history. Mum had a great love for the Queen and Royalty, perhaps because of her great respect for rules and authority. The edicts and commands of others gave credence to her own multitude of household dictates. Dictates, if obeyed, would bring order to her world.

'Where would a country be without a monarch?' Mum said, pulling on her best gloves.

'Pretty much the same place, I'd reckon,' Dad said, with sarcasm that was not lost on Mum.

'People would just blow with the wind,' Mum said.

Because Dad was often accused of precisely that, he didn't miss the point, but unlike Mum, he was greatly amused by her haughty pronouncements. He knew if the discussion followed its usual path they would end up at their ancestry. This destination was to be avoided at all costs by mum, due to numerous family legends trotted out on various occasions about Dad's family coming from aristocracy and Mum being the descendent of convicts. These caused Dad great amusement and goaded Mum into pithy diatribes on the ability of her ancestors to 'at least know a good day's work when they saw it—not like some.'

None of this offended Dad in the least. He would be inspired to bring up the story of Lord Someone-or-other who had been a botanist with Captain Cook on one of his voyages. Mum would swiftly brush this aside.

'Typical—some Lord Muck sitting around drawing flowers instead of getting on with it.'

Mum fussed over my brother, Peter, dressing him in his Sunday best. At three he was reserved, and hated to be the centre of attention, much less instigate any kind of fuss, so Mum was sure he could benefit from this historic moment. She'd been up at the crack of dawn, and was wearing her best hat and gloves.

She eyed Dad in his work clothes with a speculative look that relegated him to the category of 'unsuitable'. He had deliberated over the news of the Royal visit the night before.

'Where's your patriotism, Max?' Mum had demanded, hand on hip. Dad hadn't answered, but pretended to give the matter earnest thought.

On the big morning and he could procrastinate no longer. He declared he would be happy to 'forego the pleasure, stay home and potter around—getting things done of course,' he added, smiling, in case he was accused of doing as he pleased and not accommodating 'other people'.

Mum waited for over four hours on King Street, Newcastle, in the boiling summer sun, among the swelling anticipation of the throng of well-wishers carrying flags and streamers. She endured this, plus the squirming protests of my brother, who had uncharacteristically 'left his manners at home', only to be eventually informed the route for the Queen had been changed and she had already passed through Newcastle.

Meanwhile, on the other side of the lake, where we lived, at least an hour's drive away, Dad heard from one of the neighbours that the train conveying the Queen was going to pass slowly through the local railway station at Morisset, a few miles from home.

Dad took off in Mum's little blue Mini Minor, still wearing the overalls he'd been wearing while tinkering in the shed, and arrived at the station to enjoy a close view of Her Royal Highness, the young Elizabeth II.

When Mum arrived home hot and disappointed, Dad told her of his marvellous good luck; he'd been close enough to see the colour of her eyes. He went on to describe what the Queen had been wearing—reportedly in some detail, with a wicked glint in his eye.

'That'd be right,' muttered Mum darkly, banging her handbag on the kitchen table in disgust. 'I could just spit chips!'

An ancestral brush with fame

My great-grandfather, Harold Brooks was interviewed and the following article appeared in the Werris Creek Advocate in 1885.

THEY SERVED PRINCES
ROMANCE OF NEW LAMBTON COUPLE

More than 50 years ago, in Paris, a pretty young English woman who had left the position of governess to the family of an exiled prince, to become lady's companion with the family of Viscount Drough, watch the coachman of Baron Rothschild, resplendent in bright livery, alight from a coach.

It was a case of love at first sight. An introduction was effected, and within a year or two the governess and the coachman were married at Brixton, England to become Mr. and Mrs. H. Brooks, now of St George's Road, New Lambton.

On the eve of celebrating the golden jubilee of their marriage, Mrs. Brooks said: "I fell in love with his breeches and boots. My goodness he did look good in his livery."

Eight children and 26 grandchildren attended the jubilee celebration on November 3.

Both Mr. and Mrs. Brooks have crowded incident and travel into their lives. As an infant Mr. Brooks was taken from England to Paris by his father, who was a dealer in horses. In France the family went through the siege of Paris, which so affected the health of one daughter that she died after the siege was lifted.

Though only a small boy at the time, Mr. Brooks has vivid recollections of the scenes of hunger and horror during the siege. Anything at all, even rats, were seized upon to appease the pangs of starvation. The starving people, he said, would fry such things in candle grease. Many died during the siege, and there were many deaths from the effects of malnutrition after it was lifted.

MET EDWARD VII

There was no money in the city afterwards, for it was all handed to the Prussians. Paper money was subsequently introduced.

The first job which young Brooks got was coachman to

Prince Chime in Belgium. Then he obtained a similar job with Baron Hirsch in Paris.

There he met the Prince of Wales, later King Edward VII, Mr Brooks drove him as the Baron's coachman, and often spoke to the Prince, who impressed him as a good sport, and a man with a sense of humour. His Royal Highness, whenever he went in for a drink, always made it a point of sending out a mug for the coachman.

Leaving the services of Baron Hirsch Mr Brooks accepted a similar position with Baron Oppenheim in Cologne and in 1884 he was coachman to Baron Gustav Rothschild. It was at this time that he met his bride, who lost her heart to him when she saw him in livery.

In the Paris Exhibition, Mr. Brooks, who had a fluent command of French, which he spoke even better than English, was interpreter for the manufacturers of famous brand of mustard.

In 1890 he came to Australia, where Mrs. Brooks had relatives. For some years he was gardener for Mr. F. G. Taylor, station owner at Terrible Vale. Later he had experience at the northern mines.

EXILED PRINCE

Mrs. Brooks as Harriet Manuel, met Prince Hassan, brother to the Khedive [Viceroy] of Egypt, while he was in England in the eighties. The Prince had been exiled from his home for two years.

After the Prince's return to Egypt at the end of his period

of exile, Mrs. Brooks, in her capacity of governess too the children on ahead to Egypt. She spent two years in the service of the Prince's household.

Leaving the service of the Prince, she went to Paris as lady's companion with the family of Viscount Drough and met the dashing young coachman to whom on November 3, 1887, she was married.

Dad and me

'You take that one,' Mum said pointing at me. 'I'm not taking her to the church fete. God only knows, she can never sit still and she'd talk the legs off an iron pot.'

I could not be relied upon to meet Mum's strict standard of behaviour, as considered appropriate for Going Out in Public, so I was relegated to Dad's care. Early in life I had become Dad's companion, like scuffed shoes bundled up and sent to charity. This duty didn't seem to bother Dad in the least. He had a much higher threshold of tolerance for my chatty personality and restless energy.

'Kid never shuts up,' my mother frequently complained.

My father Max was a handsome man, tall and spare of frame with twinkling eyes that set off his gentle face. His jet black hair had receded early, lending him a professorial air. With a serious nature he was deeply committed to his spiritual convictions. He was thorough and patient, cautious and cool-tempered.

Having indulged in his share of mischief as a child, he had matured into a quiet and thoughtful adult. His humour was dry and ironic, bordering on sarcasm. Being a technical genius he designed machinery that was flawless in detail in his job as foreman at The Workshop, and then designer, in the large food processing factory nearby. He often repaired things for other people in his own time, usually without expectation of payment. Generous to a fault, he simply enjoyed using his skills to help others, chatting while he worked.

One day, he smilingly brought home a pumpkin after a long day's 'work' setting up a complete sound system for a neighbour. This man was the richest man in town and he had repaid Dad with a vegetable. A vegetable that held no particular appeal to Dad, and this caused him great amusement. Mum was disgusted to see Dad undervalued and said so in no uncertain terms. It was one occasion I was in complete accord with her sentiments.

Dad was gentle with Mum and with us. "Softly, softly, catchee monkey" was one of his phrases, one of his maxims. I loved Dad's company as much as he did mine. We were often inseparable, especially when I was older and could hand him tools as he renovated the house. This companionship usually pleased Mum, but I can remember one day when I had been particularly vocal in singing his praises.

'You think your father can do no wrong, but let me tell you, when you were a baby he never changed your nappy or got up to you at night,' she muttered with some exasperation.

Devastated at this seeming neglect on his part, I went straight to him and asked if this were true. He told me men can be a bit hopeless about knowing what to do with small babies and it was true he didn't change my nappy or get up to me at night when I was a newborn. He said it took a while to get used to me, but when I began to talk to him and bring him crushed flowers, sit on his knee and sing to him, his heart ached with wondering how he had ever lived his life before me. However, I later learned later he had often fed me when I was a toddler, because I was prone to 'blow raspberries' while eating my pureed vegetables and mushy Weet-bix. We had both been banished outside along with the high chair, with Dad admonished for 'encouraging the child in that filthy habit by laughing at her.'

Dad often took Peter and me to Newcastle harbour and showed us the tugs, ships and industrial sites. We jumped along the rows of huge bolts on the timber docks lining the foreshore, while Mum went shopping. I could never turn down the opportunity for a stroll along the harbour with Dad. Dad's brother, Ken, lived at Stockton and sometimes we caught the ferry to visit him and Auntie Em.

Newcastle was the only city experience I had for many years. The smells of the dock were just like the shed, and I loved it there. I was enchanted with the harbour and the BHP Steel Works. We had a better view of its inner workings because Dad would start a quiet intelligent chat about the mechanics and engineering side of the business, and before long we were escorted around the furnaces and the whole steelworks.

The place was alive with red-hot or white-hot metal, sparks, acrid smells and the clang and clatter of steel on steel. We heard the hiss of the molten steel as it was poured from its large steel bowls and then cooled by water. Men in their steel-capped boots were astride high metal scaffolding with their cheerful grimy faces, their hard hats and tool belts as they tended the furnaces, as agile as monkeys in trees. The huge building rang out with their hoots, laughter and the clink of the tools, while they wiped their faces with an ever-present cloth that was tucked into their belts or pockets.

I visited later on a school excursion, but it never quite lived up to the magic of those visits with Dad, where we felt like privileged guests, when the foremen treated Dad like a visiting dignitary, although he'd never even requested entrance.

Later, after the BHP had closed down I saw the dance company, the Tap Dogs, perform and was taken immaculately back to the magic and rhythm of the steelworks.

Dad would point out the container ships, and tell us all about what they carried and of the distant ports where they were bound. Exotic places, ships and workingmen fired my imagination.

He never tired of explaining or answering questions. He was my most diligent teacher and steadfast friend.

I don't need another hero

No sister ever had a more patient, reliable brother. Even though we lived in a small country town in the Sixties, many dangers still lurked. What with red-belly black snakes, sneaky boys who might ride you off the path with their bicycle or take a whack at you at school—it was a jungle out there! But what did I have to worry about when I had Peter? Calm gentle Peter, who protected, and included me in all his childhood adventures.

Even though I claimed to be an unpaid slave when he told me I couldn't be a pirate, because I had to be something else. He must have annoyed me at times because I can remember chasing him around the house, accusing him of various offences. Being older and much bigger than me, he certainly wasn't running away, merely enjoying the entertainment afforded by a little sister he could goad into a torrent of words or rash action. He would wait, let me catch up to him, then turn with a cheeky grin and say, 'Now whatcha gonna do, Sis?' The answer, of course—nothing.

He would hold me down on the hot cement path at the side of the house, declaring he wouldn't let me up until I gave in and said "uncle". One day I was provoked beyond human endurance and punched him in the nose. Down he went with a splash of blood, splayed dramatically across the front porch.

'Mum! Dad! Help! Help!' I ran into the house screaming, 'I killed Peter! I killed Peter!'

When Mum, Dad and I arrived back at the scene of the homicide, the victim of the heinous crime was grinning broadly—so I threatened to kill him all over again.

Yet he was patient; even if sometimes gratingly, righteously patient. Once, after he had tormented me, I chased him around the house for ages, which of course meant until he was bored and slowed down to look for something else to do. He smiled a slow insolent smile, enraging me further, so I threw the half-eaten apple I was munching at him. It hit him square in the ear. Then I ran. Like hell did I run!

He chased me one way, and then went around the house the other way, so that when I arrived gasping at the front of the house, there he was cool as a cucumber, waiting for me. He leant on one of the poles at the front of the house, arms folded, grinning that grin again. By then I was well and truly sorry I'd started anything, but wild horses wouldn't drag an apology from me. He walked nonchalantly past me and said mildly, 'Good shot, Sis. Glad to see you learned a thing or two from me.'

I opened my mouth and shut it.

Even though he had mates, I was often there as well to help him. He tied planks to inner tyre tubes he'd nicked from under the house of a few doors down, using ropes he'd 'borrowed' from Dad's shed. Those tyre tubes were from trucks, and made fabulous rafts. Peter was truly the son of an engineer. Not for him the simple joy of jumping in and out of a tyre floating in the creek, like the other children. He devised elaborate plans to join several together for a huge six-man raft that would take us from one end of the creek to the other. This journey was only possible after a really good rainy season. Otherwise it wasn't long before our latest transport would come aground in the shallows, or become tangled on jutting tree branches that were part of the creek's constant landscape.

When the other kids in the neighbourhood wanted a war—we gave them one. While they shot puny arrows over our fence we hurled magnificent missiles that would have done credit to Alexander the Great. Peter found a patch of thick clay halfway down our huge backyard. It was pliable enough to cut into squares with Mum's best kitchen knife, also 'borrowed', but hard enough to stay in cubes. These sat nicely in the huge slingshot he'd made from tyre tubing and they flew through the air, landing with stunning accuracy on our 'enemies'. It was always good to be on his side in any gangland war of the local small-fry. Even if I only ever handed him thick slimy missiles, then ducked when he said 'duck'.

Peter taught me about life. Necessary things your parents don't seem to cover. Stuff like how to stop boys hitting you. I remember a few balmy summer days when there were no wars or creek adventures. He wasted a valuable afternoon when he could have been lying in the hessian hammock he'd made, but instead he chose to educate me in self-defence. My ability to catch on to pugilistic techniques was very limited. His patience must have been sorely tested, but he never showed it. He ended up showing me a "good right hook" to be followed by a barrage of fast punches of any kind. 'If some awful boy hits you, keep hittin' him 'til he's lyin' down and can't get up to hit you again,' he said.

Until he went to high school we were in the same small primary school. There were only about 150 kids, with two linked playgrounds. The school was on a corner block, so all areas of the school were easily visible except behind the shelter shed. It was an established fact that anyone who went there was 'up to no good'. This sounded sinister, so I never went there. I can remember times when I was being pushed, hit or bullied, when Peter arrived from nowhere like Zorro and thumped the offender roundly. 'Leave my sister alone!' he would warn, along with threats of future visits if they didn't stop. I once had the ingratitude to say to him after he had gallantly rescued me, '*You* don't always leave me alone, you big lout!'

'Shut up, Sis,' he said, wandering back to his mates.

There was a vast area of bushland all along the nearby creek and we knew its dusty paths well. I always walked behind him chattering. I once complained it wasn't nice walking behind in his dust. Then, one day we came across a brown snake warming itself on the track ahead, and Peter quietly told me to stay behind him as we waited for the snake to move on. He calmly kept walking. I followed, heart thumping erratically, in awe of his courage. I wanted to go home and lie under the bed for weeks, possibly longer. My throat was thick with unshed tears, but I said nothing to my hero. He would only have looked at me in disgust and called me a 'girl'. Then I would be compelled to retort, 'But I am a girl, stupid!'

'You're not a 'proper' girl,' he'd say. I'd fume, wanting to whack him. I was a proper girl, what was wrong with him? 'You're better than a girl,' he'd add, making things right. If he saw tears welling in my eyes he would say 'Oh give it up, Sis,' with typical male discomfort.

In our small community a few of the kids were of Mediterranean descent, Greek or Italian. They were teased and hated being called 'Wogs' or 'Ities'. However Peter and I, with our jet black hair encouraged the myth we were Italian, although we were fifth generation Aussies with only English or Irish to claim as ancestors. If asked to speak Italian, Peter murmured any old gibberish, but because he was tall and impressive, no one argued, although they never looked convinced.

Of Danger and Dunnies

Like most other families in our street we had an outside dunny for many years. I was about twelve when we became the proud owners of an inside toilet. Ever after Mum resolutely refused to discuss the subject of dunnies. Whole family gatherings could become quite tense affairs, if one of our unsuspecting cousins happened to casually remark that no matter how poor they were as children, they were at least spared the indignity of the outside dunny. My brother and I learned to leave the subject well and truly alone in public although we had many a chuckle on the side.

The outside dunny prepared you for life in ways that an

inside toilet could never achieve. The mere act of venturing outside in the middle of the black night was enough to give courage to the faintest heart—or added fear to the already terrified soul, deeming a chamber pot under the bed a necessity. There was never a 'pot' in our house.

'I'd rather crawl through hell on my hands and knees than own one of those things,' was Mum's pithy denouncement. I was quite pleased with this decision on her part due to my propensity to 'put my foot in it' in so many other areas of life.

So we took the path of fear. The danger of meeting a snake or a red-back spider, or tripping over something and landing headlong in the dunny hole, filled me with utter dread.

I tried to carry and manipulate a torch, but while ensconced on the seat, which often moved and pinched my bum, it was very difficult to control the beam of light. At night, my terror often had me squatting near the back door in the light from the kitchen window to pee on the grass. This proved quite satisfactory until one night, Peter's dog Snoopy, arrived quietly and showed his pleasure at finding me by licking my bum. I leapt ten feet in the air, barely managing to smother a scream. This event scarred me for life. My deep humiliation was only dissipated by the fact that for once in my curious and inelegant childhood I didn't have an audience or punishment. I went back to the dunny, the torch, and my fears of the local wildlife.

Because nearly every house had a dunny, up and down the street variations of these nightly scenes of flashing torch lights and barking dogs were common. In the daytime we all rushed there as quickly as we could, when we thought no-one was watching in order to get to our destination undetected. The ultimate humiliation possible was for some neighbour to call out 'yoo hoo!' just as you had gotten up a bit of speed toward the dunny and were hiding a roll of toilet paper in your apron pocket. Because there was little entertainment to be had, it seemed people spent an inordinate amount of time in their backyards taking notice of what everyone else was doing. There were tenants to add to the number of gawkers.

Everyone in our small town seemed to rent out some part of their house, and we were no exception. Our house was divided in half and another family lived on the other side. The outside dunny was the only thing we shared—hence the only thing out of my mother's control. I remember her long monologue on an over-warm Sunday, on the proper and appropriate use of toilet paper, and her inability to comprehend why some people 'couldn't wipe their bums with one or two sheets.'

At four years of age I was already a budding diplomat and set out to sort the matter. Knowing Mum's blunt approach usually had people bruised and bloodied, I opted for the gentle approach. I lied. I politely approached the lady of the half-house. 'Could you please stop using Mummy's toilet paper, because Daddy gave it to her speshally for her birthday.'

This caused a great outpouring of mirth of which I was only too delighted to be the cause. On reflection it may have been my first successful diplomatic mission, although I can't remember if it actually solved the problem I was intending to fix.

Typical of me though, I was happy to have survived the ordeal without offending anyone.

Of course, there was the added benefit of being thought of as 'a funny little thing, where does she come up with these things'—a talent that has carried me through life, and gotten me out of approximately as much trouble as it has gotten me into.

I want to cuddle a Koala

'I don't like the zoo!'

I practised my best pout.

'Don't be silly,' said Mum, 'you love animals.'

'Not wild ones.'

My mother sighed. 'I don't know what's got into you today. Every other child loves the zoo. We're having a lovely day out with family.'

'There's too much walking,' I moaned. 'Why did we take the rail car downhill when we got here instead of uphill after walking all day? My legs have a headache.'

'Don't be, silly,' said my Peter, who was rangy and athletic even at eight.

'Stop arguing, you two. We'll have lunch soon,' said Mum.

'You said that an hour ago,' I said, sitting down on the worn pathway.

'Rubbish. Don't exaggerate. Get up, Linda. We'll find a nice picnic table and get the picnic basket out...'

'I hope you didn't make pineapple sandwiches. They'll be horrible and soggy. I don't know why we can't buy fish and chips like normal people,' I said.

'You're not normal,' said Peter, earning a sharp look from Dad.

'We're saving money,' said Mum.

'We'd save more money if we stayed at home,' I mumbled.

'At least you didn't have to carry the picnic basket,' said Peter.

'I think we'll have lunch on the blanket,' said Dad. 'I'm hungry too.'

'We can't eat on a blanket, Max. I brought salad; and peaches and custard.'

Dad looked startled. 'No wonder this Esky weighs a tonne. I'd have been happy with a Vegemite sandwich.'

'I heard that, Max,' said Mum. 'It's bad enough that the kids are complaining, without you joining in.'

'I'm only thinking of you. It would make your life easier.'

'It would make *your* life easier, you mean, Max Don't pinch your sister, Peter. Stop squealing, Linda. Alright, we'll eat on the ground like heathens! I don't know why I slave over the lot of you. Ungrateful mob. Don't blame me if things spill.'

Dad put the Esky down and unfolded the blanket.

'We can't stop here, Max. We'll be in the road.'

'Not if we eat fast,' said Dad.

'The more we eat the less I'll have to carry back,' said Peter, to no-one in particular.

I picked at my food. I loved salad, but parts of the lettuce were frozen from being next to the ice, the carrot sticks were woody, the tomatoes were squishy and when Mum opened a tin of pineapple I nearly heaved. 'Not on salad!' I begged, as Mum placed a slice of tinned pineapple on her plate.

'Ha, ha,' said Peter.

'I want to be sick,' I said. 'I can't eat anymore.'

'Mum! She's only doing that so I have to carry more,' moaned Peter. This statement was ignored, so he set about eating as much as he could, concentrating on the tinned food. 'I like the zoo,' he said, glaring at me.

'You just liked seeing the monkeys throw pooh at each other.'

'Mind your language, Linda,' said Mum.

Dad gagged on his lunch.

'What I am I supposed to call it?' I asked.

'Max! It wouldn't hurt you to back me up with the children.'

'Kid's got a point, Else.'

'How can you each so much, gobbledy guts, when you ate half the peanuts for the monkeys?' I was astonished at the amount of food my brother was putting away.

'I'm a growing boy,' he said, patting his stomach. His superior height was a point of pride. He was taller than all the boys in his class. I was four and had already earned the nickname of 'pocket rocket'.

'So?' I said.

'I have lots of muscles.'

'Well, why dontcha use 'em and stop grizzling about carrying the basket?'

After lunch I felt better, not only because of lunch, but because the stage of unpacking, eating and cleaning up after the picnic had been so time-consuming it gave me time to rest. I was also relieved that Dad and Peter were going off by themselves. Peter was excited to have an elephant ride. I took one look at the large beast and hid behind Dad. Mum took my hand. I smiled up at her – happy to have time with her.

'When will we see the Koalas?' I asked. 'I love them. We can cuddle one, can't we Mum?'

'Yes, darling, but we have lots of other things to see first.'

'I'm sorry I've been whingey, Mum.' I squeezed her hand. 'It was a long way to come to the Taronga Zoo, wasn't it, Mum? It was hours and hours and hours on the train. It was great fun going down to the bottom on the... what was it... the bumpy railcar thing...? It's was a very steep hill going down wasn't it, Mum? I thought we'd fall into Sydney

Harbour. I don't like heights. You like heights, don't you, Mum? That's why we stop at every lookout when we go on holidays. I don't like lookouts. Peter always pretends he's going to push me off. It was so exciting seeing the giraffes. What are we going to see next?'

Mother sighed. 'I really want to see the birds, Lindy Lou.'

'That's alright, Mum. You should have a turn.'

We passed bold, colourful Toucan's, elegant Flamingos, and fluttering flocks of Rosellas.

'But... but... Mum, why can't those birds fly way up high in the blue, blue sky? That's what I would want to do if I had wings. I'd fly way over the clouds.'

'They have to be in cages.'

'Why?'

'So we can see them.'

'But I don't think they want to see us.'

'You're a funny little thing, 'Lindy Lou mine'.'

I laughed. I loved it when Mum called me that.

Finally, we arrived at the Koala enclosure. A tall keeper – a blonde girl with a bouncing ponytail brought a Koala.

'Ooh!' I was excited beyond words. The Koala was much bigger than I thought – why it was nearly as big as me!

'Take her very carefully,' said the keeper, 'she has long claws and must be handled very gently.'

I held the Koala as I was shown. Forgetting weariness I reached for the blinking Koala. 'Wouldn't she rather be in the bush?' I asked.

'Koalas can have a hard time in the bush. Of course that where it's best for them, but with bushfires and floods they have a tough time surviving. We have a special program here for Koalas – we put them in families and help them keep safe so they can have baby Koalas. It would be really horrible if all the Koalas were lost.'

'Oh dear, does that ever happen?'

'Yes, some animals have become extinct. That means there are none left because they couldn't survive.'

'Oh. So extinct is when something's all gone.'

'Yes, you have it! Clever girl. Have you enjoyed the zoo?' asked the keeper.

I worried my bottom lip with my teeth. It was always so hard to say the right thing and this lady keeper was so nice. 'I... I like *this* bit, but I cried when I saw the polar bears – I mean Koalas are used to Australia, and the hot, hot, hot, but polar bears must be such a terribly long way from home where it's cold. I told Mum that it was horrible that they didn't have icebergs and Mum said the cement was painted white, but I think the polar bears know the difference and they must be very sad; and very *hot* here.'

The keeper smiled and took the Koala. Mum blinked and put her arm around me.

'We're going home now, Lindy Lou.'

Wanna go out?

'Do you wanna be my boyfriend?' asked Imogen, all coy charm, as she wriggled closer to a boy on the long lunch bench. She tugged at a stray piece of fine blonde hair, tilted her head and smiled shyly up at George, the boy next to her. She was eight. I sat across from them. We were eating lunch on the long bench seats in the shelter shed at school.

'Oorrgghh, what d'ya mean?' asked George. He eyed his sandwiches, assuming this girl's sudden presence beside him was the precursor to the usual lunchtime food swap. He wriggled a little uncomfortably, then scratched his head.

'You know, go out with me. Be my boyfriend...'

George looked confused, but Imogen was gazing into his eyes with all the practiced charm of a courtesan. 'Sure, why not,' he said, shrugging a shoulder and returning to his sandwiches. Imogen sat with him through lunch and then waved him a cheery 'bye' when he went to play cricket.

'I'm going out with George,' she said, when he'd gone, suddenly appearing to notice my existence.

'Oh yeah? Where y'goin'?' I was confused as George.

'Nowhere silly! Just out.' Imogen rolled her eyes at me.

'You're the silly one,' I said. 'How can you say you're goin' out with someone when you're not goin' anywhere?'

Imogen rose with a sigh, obviously tired of trying to get anything through my thick head. Besides, she had spied a group of other girls who were already in a giggling huddle and would greet her acquisition of a boyfriend with befitting awe. She sat with George through lunch for a couple of days, then he caught the flu and stayed home for a few days.

'So you wanna be my boyfriend?' Imogen asked, sitting next to John as he worked his way through his lunch.

John was mad about sport and wanted to finish his lunch so he could play. He was louder and more confident than George. I felt sure he would be immune to this trick, but the following conversation was alarmingly similar to the one I'd witnessed a few days ago—except I kept my mouth shut, and Imogen put her nose in the air, studiously ignoring me. She sat with John for a few days.

George returned to school. After watching for a millisecond, he saw John was holding Imogen's hand. 'What are ya doin' with my girlfriend?' he asked angrily, dropping his lunch box and raising his fists.

'What d'ya mean your girlfriend?'

'She asked me.'

'No, she didn't! She asked me.' John realised George meant business and stood to face his opponent. He couldn't back down. Although smaller, he had his schoolyard pride to consider.

'Did not!' yelled George, beginning to look confused because Imogen was standing silently near her friends. A glance in her direction gave no reassurance.

'Did too!'

By the time the conversation was this far advanced, any social niceties had been well and truly jettisoned and the two boys had taken to each other, fists flying.

'Teacher, teacher!' Imogen screamed at the top of her voice. 'Ooh!' She wailed and wrung her hands, then shrunk trembling against one of the girls. Mr. Dunn came rushing over, holding his half-eaten lunch.

'Here, you two! What's this ruckus about?' he asked.

'The boys are disgusting! They're fighting!' squealed Imogen, the boys were thrashing around in the gravel with an ever-growing audience of boys cheering them on, and girls clucking in distaste. Imogen, now a waterfall of tears, shredded a tissue, while her band of sympathisers patted her encouragingly.

'Well, boys. What have you got to say for yourselves?' said Mr. Dunn. The rough sound of his voice was enough to startle the boys out of a fight that was already losing momentum.

'Nothin' sir,' said both boys, looking down at their torn filthy clothes and hanging their heads. Mr Dunn knew he would get nothing more so he dispatched them to pick up the schoolyard rubbish together. He had an afterthought and turned to me.

'What was that all about, Brooks?'

'Imogen asked them both to go out with her,' I said, then flushed red as Imogen gave me an icy stare. 'But they weren't really goin' anywhere,' I added lamely, attempting to undo what I'd said.

Life on the creek

The creek flowed through our small country town, shuffling and groaning the whole length of the village and beyond. It was mud-thick most of the time, with sage-green mossy sticks and crumbling brown logs emerged unevenly all over its still surface, except at the widest parts.

Any ripples gentling the surface could be attributed to the furling of summer breezes, rather than any life force inherent in the stodgy creek. If young rivers are straight and true, this was an ancient and ponderous one and very few sections were free of snaking curves.

Truth be told, the creek was quite ugly and unappealing up close. But to us children, it was magic. Part of its attraction was that it was the only water available to jump into on long hot summer days, when ripples of heat shimmered off the tarred roads. The luxury of a swimming pool was unknown. The closest other access to water was at Lake Macquarie, a large salt-water lake, but visits there were rare indeed. Occasionally, during school holidays a day at the beach meant a swim in the ocean or in the protected Newcastle Baths an hour away, but that meant packing, transport and time. Things our parents could little afford.

For us, there was rustic charm to the old wandering creek. We thought it marvellous to swim in the cool shaded water, where the spreading eucalypts met and the sting of sunburn was unknown. We weren't even deterred when we sank knee-deep in clinging black mud at the reedy edges of the creek, for here we were heroes in our own stories.

We were bands of marauding pirates or seafaring explorers. Slowly gliding down the creek on rafts made of old tyre tubes or planks tied to 40 gallon drums, we were transported to the world of Huck Finn and Tom Sawyer.

On the bends or where the creek was widest, there were rope swings where the shrieks of childhood filled the summer air with life. While we were frolicking in the creek, we could forget that we were Johnny or Susie, who peddled our older sibling's bike down to the corner store with a crumpled shopping list, spending most of the journey in tears in the gravel.

It was a golden time with few responsibilities of the

modern kind. The call of your grumbling stomach told you it was time to go home for tea. There were no swimming classes, footy clubs or sporting events of any kind. Exercise and 'personal development' involved cycling with noisy groups of friends. In summertime, life for children revolved around the creek—swimming or launching themselves from thick, knotted ropes suspended from gnarled and generous gums that bent and submitted to the play of children, whose voices echoed brightly, skin slicked wet and shining.

The most incredible part of this parade of summers, according to modern dictates, was the fact that the whole experience was devoid of the presence of adults—apart from the occasional parent who wandered the bank, sat in cardigans on blankets, or horror of horrors—called out to you. This parental attention landed you with the humiliation of being branded a 'sook' of the highest order; resulting in much tantrum throwing and storming to bedrooms. The ensuing social rejection could not be lived down in a single summer.

The swing bridge was a suspension foot-bridge spanning the creek at its widest point. It was hardly ever used by adults, except as a short cut. To us it's most important function was to provide a platform for that essential childhood ritual—'Showing Off'. To be able to cross it effortlessly on foot without grabbing the cables for support was a masterpiece in balance and discipline. The ability to get from one side to the other without swaying the bridge was a sublime achievement, and gained the glowing respect of the others.

However, the ultimate accolades were reserved for those who could ride their bikes from one side to the other without mishap. Of course those too afraid to cross its swaying course alone, earned the stinging insult of being a 'Mummy's boy!' And if any of the girls could achieve this feat they were regarded as honorary boys.

Sunday School Blues

My young life was blighted. Our hairdresser must have previously worked for the military. Every day was a bad hair day. I wasn't permitted long hair like most of the other girls. Mum's excuse was that I possessed too many 'cow licks' and this affliction meant I would spend my life with bad hair days and a short haircut.

I think the real reason was that the high maintenance manoeuvres necessary for looking after long hair on a pre-schooler were beyond her talents and patience. Our hairdresser, while not actually using a bowl, managed to give me a bowl haircut every visit—a crooked one at that.

After seeing Pollyanna, I was green with envy. I dreamed about long hair and wide hats with ribbons down the back. I wasn't allowed a hat either.

I coped with the shame—most of the time.

While wandering with my brother in our neighbourhood, I didn't think much about it. The kids in our street were predominately boys and my efforts to get them to play with my dolls called down scorn, even though I accommodated them by playing with their stupid cars in the dirt.

I was often referred to as 'that cute little tomboy' by those who were unaware of my secret longings for lace gloves, ribbons, socks with bobbles, long hair and darling little purses.

I survived the embarrassment until The Lord's Day came around. They say religion changes everything. And Sunday School was the place where I stuck out like a sore thumb. After copious begging, tears and promising to be good for the rest of my life, Mum relented and bought a purse. There would be no compromise on the matter of hair, but it was still a victory. I was soon the proud owner of a purse I'd fallen in love with at first sight. It was adorable. I sashayed into Sunday school swinging that purse as if I was a model with a thousand dollar designer handbag. I made a great show at offering time, when the basket went down the rows for us to donate our freewill gift to the less fortunate. I accepted with demure grace all compliments that came my way. Oh the joy!

Pride cometh before a fall. And fall I did.

On the way to the car after the service Mum looked at me as if something was odd. This wasn't unusual. I adopted my usual nervous chatter aimed at covering any defect that might be glaringly obvious to others, but I didn't have a clue about.

'Where's your purse, Linda?' asked Mum.

My heart sunk to my feet. It was gone. My stomach churned. I hopped from one foot to the other. Tears of despair flowed down my face. At my obvious distress, Mum withheld the lecture that usually accompanied my misdemeanours. We searched the Sunday School building, the road, the church, the gutters and asked the teachers and other children. I was in agony. Mum, who was renowned for never giving up, finally had to pat my grief stricken face and tell me we couldn't do any more and had to go home. She would contact the church lost property office through the week.

I prayed. Knowing God was more inclined to listen to the penitent, I began with a list of my faults.

This alone made for a long supplication. I then expressed the things I was grateful for, my cat, a warm bed, food, Mummy and Daddy, oh yes, and even my brother although he tormented the life out of me. I then promised God I would be good for the rest of my life, hoping this impressed

Him more than it impressed my mother, who regarded me with dubious looks whenever I made this devout claim to her. I couldn't really blame her scepticism, as this dramatic outburst was usually made before a particularly undesirable punishment was in the offing.

All to no avail. I grieved openly and without restraint, throwing myself on my bed. This was something new for me, and Mum was confused by this outpouring of emotion. After much contrition on my part and dire warning on hers, she bought another purse.

It was far less ostentatious. I bravely hid my disappointment. I would not throw a tantrum. My one and only attempt at tantrum-throwing had brought such a swift and undesirable reaction that I'd vowed never to repeat the performance. I grovelled with gratitude, promising I'd never let it out of my sight. It was only for church; surely I could keep track of it for a few hours a week. But no. The same scenario was repeated the following week. Mum's patience began to wear thin.

'How the blazes can you lose something in such a short time?'

I was as puzzled as she. The harder I tried to remember, the more anxious I became. The more anxious I became, the less I remembered. Disastrously the pattern continued until I was a nervous wreck and Mum had had enough.

'You don't deserve a blooming purse if you can't keep track of it,' she said, upon arriving 'at the end of her tether'. I hung my head. I deserved no less.

This left the problem of where to carry the offering. I was

inclined to forgo the offering basket, but this opinion was not shared by my mother. I was exhorted to think of the less fortunate. I was not inclined to do so. In my opinion I was The Less Fortunate. Besides, God had not been forthcoming with helping me find my purses—find my memory, or find any possible thieves who were preying on me (one of my more imaginative scenarios).

My ever practical mother came up with an ideal solution.

Ideal *for her*.

She tied my offering coins in one of Dad's handkerchiefs and safety-pinned it to the front of my dress for the world to see. Whether she thought humiliation would stimulate my brain, or was simply solving a problem still mystifies me. So there I was; social leper, with a dodgy haircut, no ribbons or bobbled socks, adorned with Dad's handkerchief and an ugly safety pin. No matter how strange fashion trends become, this look will never be adopted by any group—Grunge, Goth or otherwise. Even at four I knew this.

If you haven't already discovered this fact, one of the hardest things to do in a hurry is untie the knot in a handkerchief while the offering basket is approaching ever nearer. Of course the usual nervous memory lapse didn't help, so my last minute panic was seen and snickered at by all. After this happened a few times I went from humiliation to anger. While walking to the car listening to Mum and Dad bask in the spiritual afterglow of a particularly stirring sermon, I kicked pebbles with the zeal that was missing from my Christian experience.

'Stop that, Linda. You'll ruin your shoes,' said Mum.

'I suppose you'll make me wear Dad's slippers then!'

'Don't give your mother cheek,' said Dad. But I caught the glimmer of a curve on his lip. I slowed down and walked a few meters behind them, dragging my feet.

'Keep that up and we'll have a talk at home,' said Mum.

'I'm not wearing Dad's stinking handkerchief again!' I blustered defiantly.

'Oh yes you will!' hissed Mum.

'I wish I was a kangaroo with a pouch!'

I Came, I Saw, I Failed

My mother saw the world in straight lines and straight answers. I was fascinated by life's twists and turns. I asked endless questions of everyone; 'How old are you? Why don't you have any little girls? Why does God live so far away? Why can't my cat talk to me? Why is it dangerous to bring any dirt inside when it doesn't hurt us outside? Who is in charge of all the money in the world?'

Mum was a domestic marvel. I guess it was quite natural for her to assume when she gave birth to me I would be just like her. I looked like her. She saw this as a good omen and rested calmly in the knowledge that her world was in order and under her enthusiastic control. For energy and motivation were never lacking in my mother.

It would be hard to discern the exact moment when she realised her practices and theories came to naught with regard to me. It was clear that God had decided to test her. She would rise to this new challenge, bringing all the energy and persistence she used to tackle the housework to this new task—the task of bringing up her daughter. But success was illusive and disappointing. None of the manuals had prepared her for me.

What confused her most was that I was not angry or defiant, I just couldn't understand or do things 'the right way' no matter how many times she tried to 'get it through my head'.

With her obsession for order Mum was always requesting Dad to build cupboards. Every room contained at least one large cupboard. Her compulsion for cleaning everything within an inch of its life included the cupboards. Unfortunately my assistance was required.

'Linda, take everything out and clean and dust the shelves.'

I was both appalled and overwhelmed. I couldn't conceive how any dirt, or even a speck of dust, could fit in with the other contents, especially under them. And I never understood why dusting was required prior to cleaning. So I usually banged around, hoping to achieve 'efficient' noises, making things look a little different. After waiting a reasonable interval I called out for her to come and inspect my handiwork. She always had to check things thoroughly. I held my breath, crossed my fingers and toes and lived in fear, until I received a grunt of approval or a swat of the back of her hand along with the inevitable, 'Hopeless, do it again!'

The linen cupboard was the biggest challenge. I think Mum bought precisely the same number of towels her family owned in the home of her childhood, when there were eight children and two adults. There were at least sixty for the four of us. When I was told to take them out to dust and clean, my fear went up several notches. This job always turned out the same. She would plunge her hand into the back and emerge with dust on it. No amount of pretending would get me out of this with my usual antics of not actually cleaning. When the three piles of towels were in the cupboard they were each a foot tall, packed firmly, taking up the whole shelf neatly. However, when removed each pile had swollen to twice their height, and grown a couple of inches wider. This phenomenon confused the hell out of me.

The cleaning and dusting were achieved relatively easily. The real struggle began when it was time to return the now larger piles of towels to the shelf. I could never do it. I squashed, pummelled, puffed and panted, but nothing on earth would make those bloody towels fit back in the way Mum had arranged them. I'd often been told the best way to manage this was to insert them one at a time. This didn't work for me. I always had about two towels left over out of each pile that just would not fit back in the cupboard.

Making matters worse, the piles now had a decidedly squashed appearance, so they didn't fit neatly, much less contain the original number. I usually gave up early as the punishment for this debacle was usually only verbal. It also gave Mum a much enjoyed opportunity to show her superiority in all things domestic in a dramatic fashion. Arriving on the signal of my much-rehearsed defeated bleating, she'd show me how it was done. With none of the panting and exhaustion that accompanied my efforts, her strong square hands compressed the towels precisely with a satisfied 'harrumph.'

Mum's pleasure with this demonstration was enhanced by my humble and grovelling praise—also much rehearsed. It was one occasion where there was no emphatic declaration of my hopelessness in all things domestic, along with her sincere wish that I'd never marry and torment some poor husband and children of my own. I like to think the towels cowered in defeat and given up, as I had. I could never repeat her skill with the towels, even after many demonstrations. I often considered throwing a few towels in the bin or donating them to the local charity on the sly.

The tortuous cleaning processes at our house also involved the windows. To be fair, they actually featured the windows, as these were most readily seen by all. Her usual method of masochism prevailed and she insisted on each window having a full set of venetian-blinds, sheer drapes and then heavy drapes.

These were all religiously positioned at precise times of the day and night. Early morning meant the opening of the blinds and pulling back of the heavy curtains. I never minded this at all as it was a ritual that gave Mum pleasure, but more importantly never involved my participation. The cleaning of the whole lot was another matter entirely. The venetians had to be removed by the tallest and most technical child, that being my father. Then they were hung from the clothes line, where it was my job to scrub every inch of them.

To add to my torment, Snoopy, the bum-licker of my previous dunny adventures, was left tied to the clothesline to add further nuisance to the task. Snoopy was Peter's 16th birthday present and his constant companion. The cleaning of the venetian blinds was high adventure for Snoopy, but caused wrath and resentment in me. No matter how pathetically I protested about his presence, Snoopy was allowed to be wherever Peter wanted him.

Mum professed to be disgusted and offended by my cats, but her death wish for my pets apparently did not include Peter's dog. Snoopy was reputed to be a cross between a dachshund and an Alsatian. Many theories on his conception were put forward and raucously chuckled over by Peter and his friends, but not in front of my mother for fear of the tongue lashing for having a 'filthy mouth'. In the genetic struggle for Snoopy's appearance it seemed the dachshund had won out. Snoopy had short legs and long ears that trailed the ground, and a furious pointy little tail. However, the Alsatian evidence was also there. He was huge, looking for all the world like a dachshund on steroids. Like most dogs Snoopy had a great and lifelong love of any kind of dirt. He was even the muddy red-brown colour of East Australian soil.

Against all logic, my mother actually appeared to have a certain fondness for Snoopy. He was allowed inside on occasion, where he nervously and energetically skidded, scraping long doggy toenails on the floors as he slipped sideways, knocking over Mum's indoor potted plants. This did not cause the same fury that was aroused upon the arrival of my cat draped lovingly over my arm when I tried to bring it inside.

To Mum, Snoopy was hilarious. Even when he ripped the edges of her best sheets, he was funny. Any complaint on my part of the unfairness of this earned me the expostulation that my cats piddled. It just wasn't worth reminding her that Snoopy occasionally left a well-placed turd on her pristine floors.

The boy who ran

One of the most vivid pictures I carry with me from my childhood is that of a boy who lived up the road from us— the boy who ran away.

Annandale Street was typical of country town roads at the time. They were slightly better than dirt tracks, at least much wider, and cars would park randomly on the gravel shoulder. The footpath consisted of a meandering dirt track that snaked the length of the street with grass worn away by bikes, billy-carts and children.

There were few cars and fewer garages. If they existed at all they were called sheds and contained far too many useful tools or junk to make space for the car. Only one family in our street had a new car and they had a double garage. We thought the bloke a tycoon. If you knew someone really well and were visiting, you were allowed to park your car up on the grassy verge outside their house. It was a public sign of the relationship between guest and homeowner.

While white sheets flapped and snapped on clotheslines on Mondays, housewives would lean over the fence to talk or go inside each other's homes for morning tea. Mum would do a little leaning over the fence, but she rejected the social niceties of morning tea. To her this was a waste of time. I remember begging for a tea-set year after year. I thought the ceremonies of hospitality were marvellous.

'You've got legs. Help yourself to some orange juice if you're thirsty. There's plenty,' she would say to us.

My paternal grandmother was a delight to have morning tea with. In a throwback to her ancestral links, she observed the aristocratic tea rituals perfectly. The milk was always poured first. I was fascinated, not just by the actual taking of tea, but by the companionship.

In Mum's world, social interchanges consisted of brisk factual conversation. Other people were discussed but not dissected. It is amazing how much of a child's knowledge of the world is learned through these informal practices, often through listening and observing, eavesdropping on the world of adults.

The women of the street watched as the boy who lived up the road ran away—over and over again. The mother of the boy was referred to by Mum as 'that poor woman'. All of the women in our street, and indeed our local church, had boundless sympathy for her. Her son was a tortured soul who would run screaming down the road and hide under someone's house, or under the supports of the corner grocery store. I overheard him described as 'having a maggot in his brain'. We never learned the nature of his mental illness. But suffer he did, and the family with him.

I had attempted to run away from home once myself, but it was an entirely different affair from Kevin's howling exit. I was ten. Mum had refused me a suitcase but allowed me a shoebox. I packed my doll, some doll's clothes and a jumper. It was a dubious rebellion. By the time I reached the front gate and saw my beloved cat I could go no further. I chose that moment to remember my warm bed and Mum's cooking, and gave up. But poor Kevin kept on running. Everyone in the street heard his comings and goings, for the journey back home was as noisy as the escape.

Kevin was ten or eleven back then. What could you do with a boy like that? His mother was an elegant, attractive woman. Every time he ran down the road she ran after him, clearly terrified, often with her apron still on over her floral gathered dress. Frantically up and down the street she ran, desperately seeking Kevin.

Often he hid for hours. His two younger sisters were pretty and feminine like their mother. Their anguish was evident by their tiny hands scrunching the fabric of their dresses as they watched the drama unfold before them.

When Kevin was about fourteen, he "went away". This wasn't talked about, never explained. Life continued as if Kevin had never existed. I still wonder what happened to him. I had watched this lovely woman dealing with a child as wild as any animal, and doing it alone. Sometimes one of the local men would help her search for her son, but not often. There were only spectators, women whispering behind hands or aprons. They shared her fear, but it was ultimately her problem.

It was the way things were done.

The haunted house at 49

The Franklin's decaying house lay abandoned. So often we neighbourhood kids had watched this house and wondered what it was like inside.

We kids had never dreamt of entering the yard, much less the house, for in our neighbourhood of middle-class society, the family seemed like wild animals. Their constant shrieking, hair pulling, swearing and unrestrained violence had us in a mixture of awe and terror. They all had bright-red tangled hair; so even before they opened their mouths they appeared untamed. The kids tumbled out of windows that had no screens and often no glass. There seemed to be a restless anxiety in them, as if they even frightened themselves.

The house itself appeared to droop in despair. We overheard it said the house was built at the same time as all the others. This confused us. As children we had no concept of the effort our hardworking parents put into maintaining our weatherboard homes. So when we looked at the Franklin house, with the paint peeling in sheets, broken boards on the walls and verandas, its appearance looked nothing short of sinister to children who'd never seen a house in such disrepair. Strange noises abounded day and night. Doors always slammed. Chairs and toys went flying out of windows and doors. Their animals crept in silent shame under the house, afraid to roam the streets like our pets, in those days before council indictments about animal ownership.

Mum, who had inherited a mixture of Irish sayings that she usually mangled said, 'They'd die of fright if they saw a brush or comb.'

The matter of grooming was not discussed by us kids, apart from the summer our parents banded together and told us to stay away from the Franklins because we'd get nits. We'd never heard of nits, but by the time this phenomenon of infestation was explained—of other living creatures sharing your hair and scalp—any thought of mixing with the Franklins died a sudden death. Not that any of us wanted their dubious acquaintance, although on occasion the older boys with their budding bravados would suggest starting a war with them.

While we took our wars quite seriously, deep down we knew that the prearranged throwing of mud over the fence, firing of crooked arrows from home-made bows, fell far short of the violence the Franklin kids regularly inflicted on each other, much less strangers. Therefore no threats ever reached the Franklin's ears. Any strutting was confined to our backyards.

We would not make war with the Franklins. Any other war meetings between the rest of us, either ended in fits of the giggles or tears, when our parents conveyed us to our victims by our ears, requiring instant and thorough apologies. I'm sure our parents knew any skirmishes between us would be forgotten by morning, but good manners dictated the grovelling rituals handed down from our forefathers. Thankfully, we'd all come from the middle-class masses or duels at dawn might have prevailed instead.

The tirades and abuse at the Franklin house went on from the crack of dawn to well into the night, with both parents seeming to have an equal share of vitriol. If our parents punished us and we were tempted to think ill of them, we remembered the Franklins and shuddered.

Then overnight, the house was empty and silent.

Our little group stood confused, but still we didn't venture near. It must be a trick. Maybe they were all sick. A few toys were strewn in the yard as if they might still be there, but there was no furniture. We'd always been able to see right through the house, because the elegance of curtains had been deemed unnecessary. Now we could see nothing inside; not even a broken chair. The house truly seemed empty. Silence reigned. Maybe the Franklins had really left the neighbourhood. We held a hasty meeting in the tree-house headquarters. Being the oldest, Peter took command of operations. It was my job to 'suss out the oldies', as I had the 'biggest ears'. I swallowed my usual retort as the whole thing had taken on the atmosphere of a military campaign. It was determined after several days and many reconnaissance missions that the Franklins had gone for good. I was satisfied and breathed a sigh of relief. We could all get back to being kids again. But no, Peter, who was either bored or had let power go to his head, declared this wasn't enough. We would investigate the empty house.

Warning bells screamed, but sadly only for me. The others, all boys, took to this idea as if it was inspired. Knowing Peter, I suspected there was worse to come. There was. For our mission to be effective we must escape the detection of our parents. Nothing would come of a campaign aborted by the oldies who had sadly long grown out of hunger for adventure and were content with a life of boredom. My heart sank. Peter claimed the only time it was possible to evade parental interference, in a neighbourhood where mothers didn't work, was at night.

I offered my opinion that parents were usually busy on Sunday afternoons, but this suggestion was dismissed out of hand as wimpy. I didn't want to go, but if I left it to the boys I'd never live down the shame. After all what choice did I have? There were no girls in the street to play with. I couldn't let the team down; even though all I wanted to do was sit by the fire with my dolls after a hot bath.

There we were, five kids from three homes sneaking up the road in the dark.

We had torches and terror. I don't remember much else. I trembled until my teeth rattled. I do remember Peter giving orders like the Arab sheiks we'd seen on the midday movies and enjoying himself immensely. As we crept through the creaking house he gave us various colourful theories about ghosts moaning in the night, seeking revenge on all who were in the wrong place. I was personally of the opinion we'd been in the wrong place as soon as we stepped in the yard, but I wasn't going to be called a scaredy cat.

When I thought we'd looked in every nook and cranny, finding enough useless junk to fill the tip, I prayed we'd go home, but Peter decided to look in the ceiling. My knees knocked in time with my rattling teeth. By this time my distress was evident. I expected a pitiful look from Peter, but instead he looked sorry for me, left me to hold the torch with the younger boys while he and his lieutenant went up through the manhole.

They came back triumphant—with a game of Chinese Checkers. To me, this was the greatest mystery of all—a family who showed all the appearance of wanting to end each other's miserable existences having a board game! I was so surprised my teeth stopped chattering long enough to declare it must have belonged to the previous owners, but the others were inclined to embellish the ghost theories.

We were all heroes the next day.

Except for me; I was a basket case.

It Takes a Village to Raise a Child

When our parents were working or busy and Peter was hanging out with his mates, I wandered the street looking for company. It was a time of safety and security. Visiting neighbours was a lifestyle, not just an occasional event—at least it was for me. While out and about I stumbled on the charm of little old ladies and their delightful homes.

Early in life I developed a love of the elderly. I'm sure this affection influenced my decision to become an aged care nursing sister. To my surprise and delight I found many old ladies were not averse to having the company of a small girl, even one who fidgeted, chatted and was curious about everything. I was warmly welcomed and although I was nervous at first, I soon felt right at home.

The universe has a way of filling gaps in our lives and these darling old ladies filled gaps in mine. I was Alice in Wonderland; allowed to wander and touch, ask and admire. The smell of old clothes and furniture became its own kind of welcoming smell. It meant sitting down at polished timber tables with starched white tablecloths. I was never slapped or reproved for occasionally putting my elbows on the table in my excitement about The Visit. I was never under anyone's feet.

There was often cool sweet lemonade made from lemons picked from trees in their own backyards. This delicious juice was kept in frosted jugs in old, round cream refrigerators. The jugs always had crocheted doilies with little beads stitched around the edges to act as a cover and keep the flies away. The juice was poured into tall, beautiful glasses. I loved the way the light was softly filtered through lace curtains and not sliced by venetian-blinds. Chairs were chosen for comfort, not function or style, and could be used by anyone, even the cat. As a devout cat lover, this impressed me tremendously. There could be no greater evidence of acceptance than having a seat just for the cat.

My elderly friends and I took little walks to the back garden where much was made of pulling a carrot or two, gentling the soil and slicing the head off a lettuce for our meal. A lazy lunch would follow, of fresh crusty bread cut in thick slices, then used to make a salad sandwich with our treasures from the garden. Things were never done in a hurry. I never encountered any tidying, but there always seemed to be order. The stories they told enchanted me completely, taking me to another place and time. I sat in the thrall of tales of an age passed, of another world. I was gently drawn into the stories of large families, love, joy and life. They wove stories of families and communities all pulling together as one, of children never lacking the company of brothers, sisters or cousins. Sitting spellbound, I learned of evenings where families sat around open fires that sparked and crackled while the women crafted quilts, crocheted edges on doilies or embroidered, making their homes beautiful by the skill of their hands. They talked of sun-browned men who snored in old comfortable armchairs, weary after long hard hours of working the land.

A couple of the old ladies had drawers full of things that were just for children. There might be an old ink-pad with stamps of flowers, trains, children playing, or animals of every kind. There were sets of colouring pencils casually produced on my arrival. It would be tempting fate to question such abundance. One tiny old lady, Cushie, as she was known to the children, lived at the end of our street. She held the most marvellous little girls' parties where a dozen of us were supplied with balloons, games and party food.

Our mothers dropped us off and we were allowed to be completely riotous for a few delicious hours.

Auntie Eileen was my favourite. She lived two doors down from us. She wasn't really an auntie, but it was considered polite in those days to call close friends of your parents, 'auntie' or 'uncle'. She would wait for me, or so it seemed. 'Well here you are, just on time. I'm just about to make some lunch. What will it be today—egg, onion and tomato again?' she'd ask on my arrival.

This was my favourite meal and I would wriggle into a tall dining room chair with delight, revelling in the aroma, and chatter to her while she cooked. I didn't pay much attention to the fact that it was often a meal just for me. She would lay out the best silver and a tray with a white linen serviette, listening intently as I jabbered on about anything and everything.

Years later, I commented to Mum how good Auntie Eileen had been to baby-sit me and feed me so often over the years. Mum was outraged.

'What are you talking about?' she said, with the voice she usually reserved for argumentative customers at the shop. 'My children never had babysitters! Never in my life did I use babysitters.'

Then it dawned on me—I had been one of the most welcome gate-crashers in history.

I remember...

I remember my first day at school. The excitement. The busy scuffle of shoes. Asphalt for miles. People in uniforms who looked like giants—the big kids. Sideways glances, the hope of friendship, the fear of embarrassment.

'Geez, they shoulda sent this one home,' said one of the boys who towered over me. 'If I was fishin' I'd throw 'er back. Look at the size of 'er. Flippin' miniature!'

We were lined up on the asphalt quadrangle.

The Rules, as declared by our Headmaster were not only achievable but immutable but inarguable. I thought of the Sunday School classes on the Law of the Medes and Persians. Then, in case our parents had lapsed in their duty we were sternly introduced to the concept of consequences. Many thoughts rushed through my mind at lightning speed. I kept those thoughts to myself. It was the only day of my schooling that I would do so.

I arrived in class and met my first-grade teacher, Mrs Borgas. She had a tinkling laugh, warm enthusiasm and moved quickly around the room. I decided I liked her very much. We were instructed to take out our writing books. I was excited to start. Then panic! Like a worried chook I began to scratch around in my bag. Something was missing. I couldn't find my HB pencils.

'I've been robbed,' I cried out.

Everyone looked at me. Mrs Borgas looked at me. Rats! I must have talked out loud, but I was upset—I was among thieves.

'Linda, you must raise your hand if you have something to say,' said my new teacher kindly.

Oh dear, I thought. The rules were going to be harder than I imagined. I remembered Mum's words as she had tried to train my errant cow-licked hair that morning, 'Don't carry on at school like you do at home.'

'Sorry Miss ... er... Missers...Teacher.' I'd forgotten her name and I went to the same church. I smiled a winning smile to make up for my glaring deficits. Mrs Borgas turned to the board and I concentrated hard on the rules and the writing. My head hurt. Chastened, I looked in my desk. My pencils were there. I'd put them in earlier. I was profoundly relieved. I really wanted to get this 'school business' right.

The boy in front of me was much better at 'The Rules'. His hand punched the air with determined purpose. The room was silent except for the scratching of chalk on board. His hand grew more frantic. Still no sound, no movement. Then, in slow defeat his hand returned to his side. There were titters of laughter around the room. The boy's legs were shaking and a yellow trickle was travelling down his chair to the floor, to form a puddle. With my eyes wide with shock I remembered thinking, 'what the hell kind of place is this?'

On my second day at school I decided I needed to take control of my own destiny. When Nature called, as surely she must, I pelted out the door to the loo. There would be no 'lolly gagging' for me on this desperate journey where I would accept no interference from teachers who couldn't even keep the rules themselves. I arrived back in the room at a more leisurely pace and was intercepted by my teacher.

'Linda, what were you thinking? You must obey the rules. You must put your hand up if you want to go to the little girls' room.'

'But you're not paying attention ... Missers ... you can't write on the board and watch us at the same time. It's not really your fault. You don't have eyes in the back of your head. Mum says she does, but she really doesn't, you know.'

I gave her a look of sympathy. She opened her mouth, then closed it. She looked tired.

'Sit down Linda,' she said. 'And do try a bit harder.'

'I will ... er ... Missers Borgas, but you know nobody can control the call of nature.'

She turned her back. The teacher had had enough instruction from the student for one day. Years later, she told me she had to turn away at times so I wouldn't see her trying desperately not to laugh. From then on I waited until I was convinced The Rules made sense before committing to them. If they did, I followed them with the zeal of a fanatic, if they didn't, I did whatever I pleased.

I continued to bolt to the loos when I needed to go, then bolted back into class. I remember thinking that surely the others would see the merit in my methods, but the idea didn't seem to catch on. Most of the others still put their hands up, which confounded me.

Some weeks later we had a "prac" teacher. Being near the teaching college made us the 'guinea pigs' for all the teacher trainees. I did my usual 100 yard dash during class and this astonished the prac teacher.

'Are you going to stop that kid? Isn't she supposed to ask?'

'No! Never mind—leave her alone. That's Linda Brooks.'

The student teacher was aghast. 'So there's one rule this kid and another for the rest?'

'Pretty much.' Mrs Borgas shrugged. 'Don't stop her. She'll talk your head off. Don't worry, she always comes straight back.' There was never a time I paid lip service to the Permission to Exit Rule for the purpose of answering the call of Nature.

My first bully

My schoolyard bully was a stout girl with ringlets and a sneer last seen on Vin Diesel. She bore an uncanny resemblance to Miss Piggy and dealt out both subtle taunts and physical torture, and her name was Janice.

I remember standing in a school line-up and being stabbed repeatedly by her with the sharp point of a geometry compass. Despite not usually being one to retaliate I reached out and twisted her thumb back—hard.

To my surprise she let out a bellow that would do credit to a prize bull. To my even greater surprise I was punished by the teachers, made to stand in front of the whole Assembly and hear a short but rousing speech on my deficiencies and the pain I had caused her.

The injustice of this came as quite a shock as Janice was at least twice my size, but the relief of being able to stand anywhere other than next to her soon overwhelmed any embarrassment, especially when I found that in my new position I could provide my schoolmates with some sorely needed free entertainment by mimicking the Headmaster's gestures as he spoke.

Over the next few years I had my mouth washed out with soap after I enquired politely of one of the teachers the meaning of Janice's latest ditty. This rhyme had apparently last featured on the lips of a drunken sailor. To my dismay I continued to suffer for going to the teachers even though they constantly exhorted us to do so. I was never sure whether the pain inflicted by her was outweighed by the punishment meted out by the teachers.

She seemed to be able to convince them I was responsible for whatever current misdemeanour was being handled that she had instigated. I must not have been very believable. Of course, I soon learned it was better not to 'carry tales' to the teachers as the unspoken law seemed to be 'shoot the messenger'.

My days of stoically bearing all ended one bright and sunny morning at Sunday School. Janice was sitting behind me. Her doting mother had gone to extra trouble with her princess this day. Her curls were shinier than ever as she bobbed her head from victim to victim. She had on a new frothy white dress and was bending her head close to mine and treating me to her newest, foulest obscenity. I snapped.

In the style of the true postal worker I went for overkill. I punched her in the nose.

Several minutes later, outside at the water fountain with her head upside down under the cold running water, howling and blubbering with the Sunday School teacher holding a handkerchief to her bloody nose I was asked in righteous tones if I was satisfied.

I was.

The Great Australian Shed

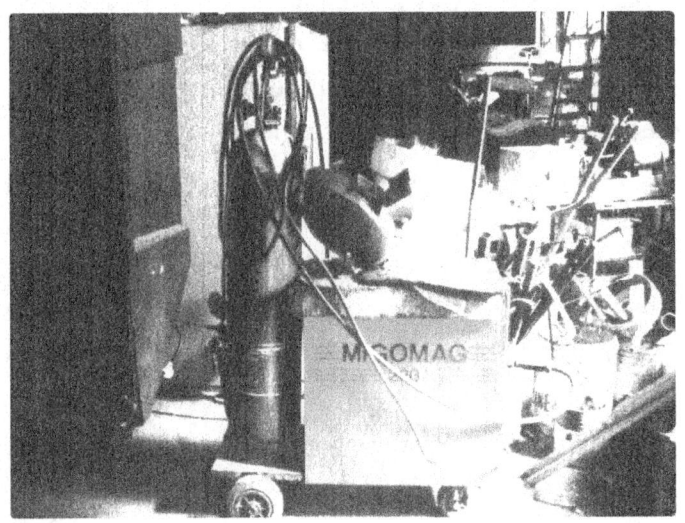

Along the journey of my unconventional childhood, I was introduced to the 'great Australian shed'. As Australians, we are excessively fond of our sheds. My theory regarding this lies in our convict heritage. After all, we arrived in this harsh land, with nothing but the chains on our feet. The ships that brought us here carried more guns and soldiers than tools. Ingenuity was mandatory. If the aristocracy had arrived without the convict element they would soon have died; manual labour was of more value in this new land than following the correct morning-tea rituals or organising a fox hunt. Of course, it's only a theory.

At first, when very young, I thought the shed was where Dad hid from Mum. Later on, I discovered that although there may have been some truth to this assumption, there was so much more to Dad's shed. It was chock full of useful tools Dad used to make marvellous things. I was constantly fascinated and often joined him there. The fact it was a place of gentle harmony added to the appeal.

Mum would get up a full head of steam to tackle the housework, taking on the mantle of martyred slavery. Mops, buckets and vacuum cleaners would appear. Dad would stand near the back door and clear his throat.

'I'm just ducking out to the shed, Else,' he'd say.

I stood next to him. 'I'm duckin' too,' I'd add, holding my breath and crossing my fingers. Escape was so near but so far. Because we were both considered hopeless at assisting Mum in the housework that began at dawn and ended at midnight, she'd let us go with a weary sigh.

Mum seemed afraid of the shed, with its smells of metal, the noise and sparks of the welding machine and the oil and grime. I remember her storming in there only once, and promptly putting her foot in the sump oil Dad was recycling. She gave us a short speech on the filth of the pair of us, and the dangers of dirt in general, but as she was discomforted by an oily foot she very soon left us to our mess. I wondered on this occasion, as I had on many others, if these incidents were not quite as accidental as they appeared, but strategies of my father to discourage her from entering his domain. He wouldn't have been the only male in history to do so. He gave no sign of this, but at times he could be inscrutable.

Dad was orderly and precise. He enjoyed his world of tools and tinkering immensely, whistling as he worked.

On the shed wall was a Masonite board with hooks and holes and the outline of whatever belonged there. In my mind the shed was a tidy place although every bench was cluttered with projects in various stages of completion, unlike inside where not a crumb was allowed to linger on floor or table. The shed was a different kind of tidy than inside the house. His tools were always in their proper place in his own system. Engine parts, gas bottles and cables were allowed on the floor, but he never misplaced anything.

Dad made wrought iron gates and trims. All our car repairs were undertaken by him, and later by my brother. There were tyres he was re-treading, deepening the groove with a hot electric thing that looked like a soldering iron. I can't even remember what it was called because I learned very little about the things he did, and much about the patient focus with which he approached each task. Dad kept his tools clean with a kerosene soaked rag. He had an old peach tin with an inch of kerosene and a rag. This was a job I often requested, just to be near him. I sat quietly on the floor making sure all the grime was wiped off his tools or engine parts.

If Mum had bothered to look, she would have been shocked to see me curled up contentedly on the rough cement floor, quietly and diligently polishing Dad's tools.

Just under the ceiling of the shed Dad had positioned

wire meshing the length and breadth of the shed. He hung lights from this in various positions to illuminate whatever part of the car engine he was currently fixing. Although this marvellous system served his lighting purposes effectively, he allowed me to think I was indispensable by holding the torch for him. I would do this for hours, shining the beam exactly where he needed it, while he talked about gearboxes and how to care for them so the gears wouldn't grind and shear off. He explained pistons, talked about carburettors and how the clutch worked. Never quite grasping his skills or passion for those things—I did learn about life and unconditional love within these lessons about machinery and tools. I learned that if you wanted something to last you had to take care of it.

Among the vices, electric saws, spanners, nuts and bolts, there were always collections of paint cans and airbrushes. Dad made signs for the church notice board and pungent paint fumes filled the shed, along with the smells of the welder. There were several soldering irons and grinders that filled the air with the smell of metal shavings and hot molten solder. It was a wonder we weren't a bit high on the cacophony of smells. We were certainly happy out there. Many years later, after his death, I visited Sovereign Hill, in Victoria and stood transfixed with unexpected tears when I walked into Ye Olde Blacksmith's.

It smelled like home.

'I'm going to teach you jolly kids manners!'

'I'm going to teach you jolly kids some manners if it kills me!' Mum announced.

It was a wintery Sunday evening. Peter and I exchanged sideways glances and smothered the urge to snicker. Mum hated snickering. She always felt she was the target, regardless of the real cause. Thinking perhaps we'd been banging the cutlery onto the table a little noisily, I quietened my efforts. My desire to please wasn't shared by Peter, who increased the decibels accordingly.

For just the four of us we were quite a noisy bunch at

mealtimes. Although Mum was fond of domestic order in the house, she seemed to love the dinner table chatter and was partial to joining our lively debates and conversations. I wondered what she had in mind.

'You've got no idea, the pair of you!' she said, thumping the casserole onto the table. Peter snorted. I snickered. 'You needn't think any of that Tommy rot will get either of you anywhere!' Mum added. Pretending I needed to rush to the dunny, I exploded with laughter.

Mum's direct approach with people was legendary. She was the manager of a grocery store. In my opinion her dealings with customers fell way outside the category of good manners. This was even more evident with Sales Reps. Mum regarded reps on a par with muddy boots—you couldn't help having them, but the less you had to look so with them, the better. I found her attitude entertaining. More often than not, I was secretly proud of her forthright style, although I would rather have been invisible at times. I used to visit her at work after school, tidying shelves, sorting fabrics or weighing vegetables—making sure I was useful.

I remember one afternoon when one of the haberdashery reps arrived, the aroma of Old Spice preceding him. This alone was enough to displease my mother. Although she held a high standard in personal hygiene, and didn't mind a dash of manly aftershave, she had no time for anyone who 'doused themselves in the stuff.'

With a flamboyant swagger he approached Mum. The staff, who knew Mum better than he, parted to allow him through. Mum's eyes narrowed as she took in his slicked-back hair.

'I told you not to come back for three months,' she stated loudly.

'Oh,' he ventured, undeterred, 'I was in the area and...'

'Nonsense. There aren't any other stores with haberdashery departments within 50 miles. You're just wasting my time.'

'Surely, it must be nearly three months,' he continued, now struggling for ground, with an ever-growing audience.

'Five weeks. That's how long it's been. Don't you keep a diary?'

So I couldn't help but feel Mum's proposal to teach us manners was doomed to failure. I remembered the countless times she'd yelled, 'What do you want?' out the kitchen window to visitors. In her book it was 'ignorant to come sneaking around to the back door.'

I wondered what had triggered the idea. She'd never been too bothered by our supposed lack of manners before. Perhaps she'd just watched the Royal family at dinner in a documentary and had been inspired—or embarrassed.

Dad's amusement was also aroused by Mum's plan. She conveyed it to him when he arrived home from work. However, unlike 'we jolly kids', Dad held his peace. The wicked twinkle in his eye was entirely missed by Mum.

'How are you going to achieve that Else?' he asked reasonably.

'What do you mean "how am I going to achieve it"? A person could do with a bit of help, Max. At the rate those two are going they'll be no better than heathens.'

'Well, of course Else—only too happy to help. What did you have in mind?'

'Meals for a start. They talk over the top of one other. When they're not elbowing each other, they put their elbows on the table. If a person was expecting a "please", they'd die waiting. And this grabbing salt and bread across each other is enough to curl your toes.'

So the lessons began. As all good teachers do, Mum outlined the rules, which might as well be 'stated at the get go'. Dad cheerfully offered to write them down and earned a look of scorn. He was showing far too much enjoyment in an idea that was serious business.

Peter and I slouched in our chairs. Slouching was instantly added to the rules.

'Oh, for crying out loud, Mum,' said Peter.

Grumbling to the cook who'd slaved over a hot stove was added swiftly.

'That's a lot to remember Else. You don't think we should start simply?' questioned Dad, justly fearing the list was getting out of control.

'They should've been doing all this for years.' Mum ground out the words. 'A person can only take so much ingratitude and bad manners.'

Being a games addict, Mum decided there should be some form of scoring. A reward for the winner. Dad's eyes grew round.

'Don't overdo it Else.'

'A person gets sick of being accused of overdoing things

when other people do nothing. A Freddo for the winner won't be "overdoing" it.'

So the game was on. Dad brought out the peg basket for keeping score. We all started with 10 pegs. Any infraction meant you lost a peg to the person who noticed your misdemeanour. Dad's face glowed. Even Peter and I were infected a sense of excitement. Never had dinner time been such fun.

The room was filled with gleeful cries, 'elbows on the table', 'forgot to say please', 'didn't ask to pass the salt', 'he slouched', 'she used the wrong knife', and so on. Even before tea was halfway through Mum noticed a disturbing phenomenon. All the pegs were in front of Dad's plate. Mum's had been the first to disappear, at an alarming rate.

'Hmmph,' she muttered.

Undeterred, she soldiered on. Night after night, we watched each other with eagle eyes. Mum concentrated so hard she got a headache. And still she was the first to lose her pegs—over and over again. Never one to give up, she put more effort into it.

'I'm not one for throwing in the towel.'

'Good on you, Else. The kids are learning fast.'

Mum surveyed Dad's face for signs of sarcasm, and finding none, she reluctantly conceded he was right. The glaring fact that she was the worst offender was not voiced. She was taking her failure with considerable grace and we kids were having far too much fun to have it end too soon. Dad's quick hand, and quiet 'you forgot' this or that, had us all on our toes. Although Mum hated to lose or be the butt of any jokes she would not give in.

Then one evening we arrived home to find dinner on the table, but no pile of pegs. Our disappointment was palpable.

'Geez, Mum. Where are the pegs?' asked Peter, forgetting for the moment that 'geez' meant the forfeit of two pegs.

'I had a big wash,' said Mum, with a voice of finality. We were gobsmacked. Mum never had washing left on the line in the evening. She even came home from work at lunchtime to take it in.

'Oh, who cares,' said Peter. 'Dad won all the Freddos anyway.'

The Great Escape

'Good grief, Dad. That looks like a whale skeleton,' I said.

'You've got an imagination there Bub, I'll give you that.' Dad continued to plane the curved boards with rhythmic precision, clearly enjoying my confusion. 'How's the surface going on that frame, Pete?'

My brother ran a practised hand over the timber. 'Feels pretty smooth, Dad.'

'Good, son.'

There was a load of washing to put on the line, but as usual Dad's projects held greater appeal than any form of domesticity. 'Can I…?'

'You'd be a help if you tied Snoopy up somewhere else, Sis,' said Peter.

'Aww, leave off! He's too strong for me. He runs round in circles, winding the chain around my legs and pulls me over.' I eyed Snoopy with reluctance, and received his usual tongue lolling grin and thumping tail greeting. 'Anyway, where'll I put him? There's only the clothesline and I have to hang the washing out.'

Peter rolled his eyes. Dad looked up, and pointed to the back step where Mum stood, hands on hips. 'Washing won't hang itself, Linda,' she said.

'Doing it, Mum.'

'You're a heck of a long way from the clothesline and basket for someone who's 'doing it', Linda,' she said.

I ran to the clothesbasket, threw it in the trolley and lowered the line.

'Forget anything Linda?' asked Mum.

'Aaaah, I don't think so…'

Mum held out the peg basket.

'Oh. Right.'

'You'd forget your head if it wasn't screwed on,' said Mum. 'Leave the men alone.'

This was usually a scenario my brother was only too pleased to join in, but he was either engrossed in helping Dad or having a day off teasing me.

Mum smiled at 'the men' with pride. Not for her the nagging of weary wifedom over half-completed projects strewn across backyards for years. Dad finished what he started. If Mum ever complained he was taking too long at anything we kids started a uproar 'Fair go, Mum. You've gotta be kidding!'

We holidayed at Eraring with an assortment of other families. Years earlier we'd gone on travelling holidays in the little round caravan Dad built, but lately we'd been renting cabins on Lake Macquarie.

We spent Sundays at Shingle Splitters, a point that jutted into the saltwater lake dividing it into a calm haven on one side and a windswept reedy curve on the other. Sometimes the wind turned, its mercurial gusts rampaging both sides, or the calm one - the side sloping gently into the lake. Cobalt-green water crimped in midday breezes as it lapped with metronomic lyric on creamy sand. Tall pines extended to the end of the point. A hilly area where eucalypts, pines and scrub gathered indifferently allowed children a secret domain, where shrieks of 'You're it, tagged ya' echoed over the water.

Then it all changed. The speedboats came with their growling engines, pristine fibreglass perfection, water thumping speeds, mile-wide wakes and spitting spray. They heralded a new kind of weekender—water skiers. We moaned that our peace was ruined, our favourite place had 'gone to the dogs'. Even Mum ceased her crossword puzzling in the shade of a tree to squint at the newcomers and mutter 'Hmmph.'

Dad got an inscrutable glint in his eye. He and Peter took off on trips to the marina at Toronto.

'Crikey, Max,' said Mum, 'you're not looking at those fancy expensive boats are you? In our dreams.'

But, come summer, we were the proud owners of a sleek speed boat with a gutsy roar, and dashing blue strip Dad had meticulously painted. It spewed smoke with the best of them.

So we learned to ski - and by that I mean Peter morphed into James Bond, while I survived as long as the boat went in straight lines, which didn't happen much. There I went - careening off at a perfect tangent to the trajectory of the boat, where I sank in ignominy and had to be pulled aboard spluttering, with my life jacket choking me.

Hospital nightmare

It's interesting how profoundly some experiences affect you throughout your life. Funny how you carry events from your childhood, as if packed in a little suitcase.

I remember being nine.

Never ill herself; to Mum sickness and infirmity was a mortal sin, brought about by some action on your part. It was always preventable. God knows how. She was personally affronted, and responded with great ire; perhaps thinking if she got upset enough it wouldn't happen again.

Once when I had become ill with chicken pox, I thought I had died and gone to heaven, because my brother and I were allowed into the sacred domain of the parental double bed. We were served food on a tray with a lace doily because both of us had succumbed to the virus. When she was convinced we were ill she took great care of us. It was just hard getting her to believe us.

The fact that we had managed to contract the disease was initially viewed with resentment by our mother, but she couldn't argue with a million spots.

One day I ran home from playing buckled over with severe stomach pain. I had run in such haste I'd left a shoe on the way. I was flushed and feeling very sick. I was interrogated thoroughly by Mum. The ensuing questions covered every possible misdemeanour and all probable causes, including the disbelief track.

What have you eaten? What haven't you eaten?

Where were you? What were you doing?

Are you bunging it on? Are you sure?

All of this was a big ask of a small girl, doubled over moaning, with one shoe missing, lost in the hurry to get home. I tried desperately to remember what I'd eaten.

'Why are you asking me this Mum? You're the one who feeds us?'

With stomach pain making my eyes water, and with a crippling fear of the unknown, I endured her questions.

Eventually deciding my symptoms might be genuine, she phoned for the doctor. By this time I was in even greater pain and hurling like there was no tomorrow. When he arrived everything began to happen in a hurry.

I wish I could say the rest passed in a haze, but it was all too clear. I became aware I was going to be 'sent away', by myself, in an ambulance. Sent to the local hospital and admitted, I was confused and terrified. The speedy diagnosis was an urgent case of 'burst appendix'.

The nurses told me I would be put to sleep. Sheer panic took over. Wasn't this what happened to animals? And then, please God help me, I would be cut open and the 'bad' taken out. I thought I must have been really bad.

I was then told to do a 'wee wee' in a container in the bed in front of the nurses. I couldn't oblige, so two nurses held me down while a third attempted to catheterise me. I screamed and kicked the instrument tray to parts unknown, scattering everything all over the floor. This upset more than the instruments, and several slaps were sharply administered.

A petite red-haired nurse, with bouncing steps and radiant smile intervened. She carried me to the toilet, explaining what was required, held a kidney dish and the task was accomplished in minutes. The same sweet nurse comforted me many times over the next week. When she was on duty, if I needed to go to the toilet my 'angel' nurse piggy-backed me rather than bring a bedpan. I loved her and never forgot her.

Alone and terrified, I was given one beneficent gift just before they came to take me to the operating theatre. The universe smiled on me. Auntie Eileen, who wasn't really an auntie at all, had had her gallbladder removed a couple of days before. I never knew how she found me, but there she was beside my bed, telling me everything would be all right.

'The doctors and nurses will take you into a big room with a really bright light. They will give you a little needle that isn't even as bad as a mosquito bite. This will make you take a nap, just a little sleep, not the kind of putting to sleep that happens to stray animals at all. Then they take the little sick part out of your tummy and you'll wake up a bit funny and sore,' she said reassuringly. 'Like me.'

The nurses let her accompany me to the theatre doors, where she planted a kiss on my head, saying she would see me real soon. 'We'll both be home again before you know it and I can make your favourite lunch,' she murmured into my ear.

Mum only visited once while I was in hospital. She sat stiffly beside my bed, clutching her big black hold-all bag tightly against her chest, afraid to touch me, too constricted by her own fears to comfort me. After only a short time, and visibly flinching at the cries of the girl in the bed opposite she said, 'I can't take this' and left. Crippled by a world where she was helpless to 'do' anything, she couldn't cope.

In visiting hours, an old man used to come and sit and talk to me. He gave me an ice cream.

'Don't you have anyone to visit?' I asked him.

'I'm a drunk,' he said, 'I can't visit my own family because they don't want me.'

'I do!'

When I cried at night the nurses hit me and told me to be quiet. I got into the habit of using a pillow to muffle my sobs so they wouldn't come. When they ordered me to get up after eight days in bed and walk all the way down the long corridor, I promptly fainted.

The absolute terror of this experience stayed with me. It probably affected my decision to become a nurse. I wanted to be like my red-haired angel nurse, but it also gave me a burning commitment to tell patients the truth, and fight for their rights to know the truth.

Cobalt princess

'I'm going to learn to sew garments. I'm taking a course at Tech,' said Mum.

It was a quiet winter evening. Three astonished faces turned toward her, Dad's, my brother's and mine. Mum and machinery did not mix. A genius at Maths and fast as lightning on a typewriter, Mum was hopeless with all things electric or mechanical. We would have been less surprised if she'd said she wanted to be an astronaut.

She had a Singer treadle sewing machine and often hemmed and mended our clothes. As a young woman she had done beautiful hand embroidery, but we were sceptical about the addition of electricity to the equation. She often complained the toaster didn't work because she hadn't plugged it in.

However, she was determined and bought an electric sewing machine, then went and signed up for an evening course at the local Technical College. She would take her sewing skills to a new level—she would do more than hemming and mending seams. In typical style she opted for the toughest assignment. She decided to make an evening garment. Already fascinated by sewing I had sat on her knee at the treadle machine, thrilled with sewing simple seams as her strong hands guided mine. I focused intensely on making straight lines, as well as maintaining the even rhythm of the treadle foot.

Excited by her new venture I watched every step. I was seven and looked at the new paper patterns with awe. This was a new world. The ability to make your own clothes, exactly the way you chose! Wearing something no one else would have, wow! And it was all going to happen right before my eyes.

Mum sat me down and told me she was learning to draft her own patterns. She showed me heavy cardboard templates that were used.

'They're a bit small Mum,' I said. 'How will you fit into that? Do you have to make it bigger for your homework?'

'I'm making a dress for you,' she said, her eyes filling

with pride. 'You'll choose exactly what you want.'

We sat and I drew a picture of my dream dress. I wanted a lace front in white, a scooped skirt over a lace underskirt, with a bow at the front. I wanted tiny, puffed sleeves. And for the dream to really come to life I wanted shiny cobalt blue. I felt like Cinderella.

Watching every step was both agony and ecstasy. I bit my fingernails to the quick.

Mum wrestled with each new stage, spending hours pinning, tacking, measuring and stitching. She said there was a fashion show at the end and I would model the dress on a catwalk. My life took on a dreamlike quality.

She stayed up late at night, muttering and struggling. One day she'd been working quietly for hours.

'Max, come here!' she called.

'Can't right now, Else.'

'Max! A person wouldn't call a person if they didn't need a person to come!'

Dad went and was distressed to find Mum had sewn her finger to the dress. He had to disassemble the presser foot and the needle to release it.

'Why didn't you tell me what was wrong?' Dad said in astonishment, looking at her blood-stained finger squeamishly.

'A person doesn't like to make a fuss over a little blood, Max.'

Dad looked like he might faint, but because Mum had the antiseptic and cold running-water well in hand, he merely patted her finger dry and applied a Bandaid.

Finally the dress was finished. It was perfection. There was a last-minute hitch on the evening before I went on.

We discovered I needed gloves, so I had to wear a pair of Mum's. This added a 'Minnie Mouse' effect to the whole look. I didn't care. Nothing could spoil the moment.

I'd practiced walking down the catwalk, head high, carefully watching the row of lights. When my turn came, my face outshone them all.

Not only because it was the first time I'd felt like a princess, but because my mum had worked so hard to make me the best dress I'd ever seen. I was so proud of her.

Everyone assumed she'd found a new passion.

'What will you make next, Mum? Will you make yourself something nice?'

I wanted her to have a reward.

'Oh heck no!' she exclaimed. 'I'm never doing that again—it's a mug's game. It's back to hems and mending for me.'

I wasn't a bit disappointed. I was her princess; if only for a day.

'Is it too much for a person to ask?'

'I want this room tidy, with everything in its rightful place,' Mum said firmly.

She stood at the entrance to my room. In her opinion, my room was 'a pigsty'. At four years of age I'd never seen a real pig much less a sty. This was in the time before preschools and televisions were common. The only pigs I'd seen in picture books looked pink and cute—they must have cleaned them up for the photo shoot. A friend who lived down the road once had a stye in her eye, but there was nothing in my room to help me make the connection, even remotely, that Mum desired of me.

'I don't want to lay my eyes on you, or this room again until it's tidy.' She turned to leave and seeing my inert expression added, 'Is it too much to ask you to put things where they belong!'

This statement rather dramatically increased the consequences and sadly also the odds on my chances of comprehension. She was calm and unbending. Her clear eyes left no room for discussion. There wasn't a shadow of doubt in her mind that not only did I understand her meaning, I was entirely capable of following her edict. I wasn't.

To me her words were the equivalent of 'When I come back into this room I want to find you speaking Chinese.'

My stomach became a tense little knot. I took a deep breath. My head hurt with the effort. I should be able to do this. Mum sometimes came to enlighten me on tidying my room. She moved around the room like a whirling dervish banging and gathering things at the speed of light. During these 'demonstrations', while she flew about like a furious hurricane it was like watching a modern teen demonstrate the workings of their latest iPod to a geriatric—it was all too fast, too furious for me to keep up with, much less emulate.

'Why you see the need to have clutter everywhere is beyond me!'

Why she categorised my treasures as clutter was beyond me. In fact the whole thing was beyond me. I fervently wished for the courage to answer her question of, 'Is it too much for a person to ask?' with a resounding

'Well yes, quite frankly.' But at four, I lacked the eloquence and courage.

On the surface it seemed simple—why couldn't I remember where things belonged? After all, I didn't have much stuff. Her system simply didn't make sense to me. I hated my room when she had tidied it, devoid of my treasures and favourite things, which were thrust roughly into deep drawers. I remember a tortured moment when I worried if my teddy and dolly would be able to breathe. No toys were allowed on my bed. The room was clinically bare. It could have been a hospital room. There were no girly touches, even in the drapes or furniture.

Quite simply, after Mum tidied my room it wasn't my room anymore. It wasn't even like her room where delicate crystal vases and baskets sat in delightful array. There was nothing of me left.

I stood in the centre of my room contemplating the tidying problem. After a few minutes of chasing the idea around my head I realised the solution was not forthcoming. I did the one thing that made sense to me. I climbed into my wardrobe. She didn't want to see me if I couldn't do it, at least I could fulfil that bit. I snuggled into a corner on top of my clothes and shoes.

'Linda!' yelled Mum, opening the wardrobe door and regarding me with astonishment. She was confused. I'd been nothing but confused for the past hour.

'I don't know where you came from,' she said in a tired voice.

Whenever she decided I was too old for a book or toy it

simply disappeared, with the most common explanation offered that it had gone to 'poor children who had nothing'. When I left home at 18, I only had a handful of birthday cards as mementos, which I'd hidden from her eagle eyes in my underwear drawer.

After I returned from having my appendix out, Mum had decided in my absence it was the perfect time for 'a good clean up'. I came home to no teddy and only one doll. She made the mistake of telling me Dad had buried them in the backyard.

She underestimated my determination, and tendency to accept at face value whatever she said. Still weak from surgery and doubled over, I grabbed a hoe and began to dig. Mum was horrified.

'Stop that Linda! You'll break your stitches!'

'I don't care. My teddy is buried alive.'

'Don't be silly, teddy's aren't alive,' she reasoned.

'Not anymore it's not!'

'You're nine. You're too old for this nonsense. Why won't you believe me?' she cried in exhaustion.

'Who's going to believe someone who lied about Santa Claus!' I ranted. Then, leaning on the hoe, I paused and gazed at her through narrowed eyes.

'Is my teddy and my other toys buried in the backyard or not?' I demanded fiercely.

She'd never seen me angry and sighed in defeat. I was obviously not going to give up. The thought of her pristine lawn being attacked by a deranged child on a mission was more than she could take.

'No, they're not, I'm sorry,' she muttered defensively. 'Your father took your toys to the rubbish tip. I thought it was time to clean out the things you'd grown out of.'

I stormed wordlessly inside, lay down on my bed and faced the wall. Then with great dignity, I soberly declared that I was never eating again.

'You can send my food to the poor children!'

A dangerous time

It was a dangerous time to live. It was a time of hurdy-gurdies, pogo-sticks, slingshots and billy-carts without brakes. Added to the death-defying aura was the fact there were no such things as kneepads, elbow pads or any protective gear. If such things had been invented, they were unknown to us. If you were lucky, your Dad tied a pillow around you as you headed to certain death down the nearest gravel slope on borrowed skates.

After all, we didn't need protective gear—our Mums had Dettol, and they weren't afraid to use it! The memory of gravel rash and the subsequent howling sting of the antiseptic would have kept us awake at night, if we hadn't been so darn tired after a day roaming the countryside. It was the Sixties.

Cycling was called pushbike riding. We didn't ride our bikes home quickly before nightfall for fears of cars even though we had no lights on our bikes. No, we rode like white lightning for fear of our parents' wrath. When Mum called the clan to tea, her weary voice parting the chill of the late afternoon air, we'd better run through the back door— or else.

Not for us the eyestrain of computer games or muscle

twitches of the recumbent. Were we bored? Perhaps, but we'd never have said so, because parents interpreted boredom as the express desire to be put to work with household chores. Televisions were like stars—they only came on at night.

The days were ours; we ruled the streets. Once our wobbling first efforts at bike riding became the steady speed of success, we were off.

Those truly spectacular riders held the honour of being able to ride across the swing bridge without stopping. There was the added peril our friends might shake the bridge as we traversed its swaying course, even though they'd 'crossed their hearts and hoped to die' that they wouldn't. Dangerous times indeed.

Many were the tears shed by inexperienced riders as the front wheel jammed between the upright suspension cables, sometimes leaving the front half of the bike dangling precariously over the edge of the bridge.

However, the applause from the other children was worth the trouble. With no competitive sports or bragging common today about getting to the next level of the latest computer game, these were our only accolades.

Our house was similar to many others of the time, in that rooms had been added in a completely random fashion, because most of these renovations were constructed without any council approval. Inch by inch the law was flouted.

Some houses had so many rooms tacked on that the original house was completely swallowed up.

The usual practice was to add a veranda, then put a roof over it and then wall it in. The same was done to carports. It was before the time when rooms were added for parents' retreats, play-rooms, teenage retreats and en-suite bathrooms.

If you needed the loo while someone else was there, you were simply told to cross your legs, shut up, and buzz off.

I remember an Indian summer when soft breezes blew. Mum was in the kitchen and she was complaining to Dad, who was 'puddling' in the yard. It was late afternoon as she warmed to her latest lament.

'I have to do everything for those children, bath them, dress them, and put them to bed.'

This indisputable fact was delivered with arms crossed.

This particular day 'those children' were too dirty to even come inside. Due to Dad's inventiveness the tap outside our outdoor laundry had hot and cold water, so we were the only kids in the street with a warm water garden hose. This is what Dad used to hose us down after throwing us a bar of laundry soap. Then, he stood back with the supreme satisfaction of one who has solved a difficult problem.

Mum's face from the kitchen window said otherwise. There is nothing quite like a bit of nervous rebellion to get a fit of the giggles going and Peter and I laughed so hard it hurt.

When Mum came outside to give Dad a piece of her mind, a rather large piece apparently, she also became a target of the warm water from the hose. We children fell about with the kind of hysteria only experienced by those seeing something supremely funny, but knowing terrible consequences, or death, might be only seconds away. Our joy was complete. It was a moment of exquisite happiness.

As I said, it was a dangerous time.

Dad's apprentice

'I'm going to build a shed,' said Dad, over breakfast one Sunday morning.

'But we've already got two sheds Daddy.' I was confused.

I had been my father's apprentice for half a dozen years. I'd begun at the age of five when I discovered my aptitude for 'puddling in the shed', as mum phrased it, was greater than any abilities I possessed for assisting order inside our pristine abode. I began, as all apprentices do, with watching, listening and fetching.

Then I had graduated to cleaning engine parts and holding the torch for Dad to see the deep and secret parts of the car engine. I knew just how important it was for the beam to be steady. There we would be—two heads bent together, wrestling with the problem of repairing tired car engines.

However, this construction of a shed was a whole new venture. My mind boggled at the thought. We had a work-shed at the back of the house. It was where all the wonders of machines, ham radios, wrought iron welding, stone polishing and sign making occurred. Then there was the 'back shed' another 100 yards or so down our half acre block, in the shade of the mulberry tree. It housed timber and kindling for the incinerator. It also contained used boards with rusty nails that we kids invariably trod on as we raced through—getting them stuck into our bare feet, or through our shoes. This misadventure would require a trip to the doctor for a tetanus shot.

Our tree-house was next to that shed and we would often lie indolently back, choosing the plumpest mulberries, while the furl and smell of the smoke would rise tantalisingly towards us. Of course, we deserted the tree-house on the days Dad burned old tyres below, where there was a permanent brown patch. Mum often lamented she'd never have lawn there. It was the only blot on her perfect grass, which was watered by Dad's complicated watering system, and she referred to it as 'a blight to the eyes'.

'Never mind Else,' Dad remarked blandly, 'less to do.'

'Humph. Less for *you* to do Max.'

Dad never disputed this fact, he merely smiled sagely.

'Why do we need another shed, Dad? Are y'starting another hobby?' Dad winced at the word 'hobby'. This was often Mum's assessment of his many skills, as if he were a recalcitrant child who had a playroom all to himself, while she 'slaved' over the real jobs.

'Ah,' Dad said, his face alight. 'This 'shed' is going to be a garage.'

'Oh my,' I said, my eyes round with wonder. 'Can I help?'

'Thought you'd never ask,' he responded, eyes twinkling.

I gulped my cereal. This was indeed an honour.

'Don't plough through your food, Linda. You'll choke,'

said Mum. 'I suppose that means I'll be getting no help today.'

I pleaded with Mum with my eyes—my words so often brought trouble.

'Oh go on, the pair of you. I suppose you'll come back filthy.'

'Of course not, Else. We'll wash up outside,' said Dad.

Mum sighed. Her idea of a proper standard of cleanliness appropriate for entering 'her' house did not match ours. We children had long ago learned the sheds were Dad's and the house was Mum's. Until repairs we needed to the house and then it was 'his'.

When I went outside. I was stunned. There was a pile of bricks, large bags of cement and an old worn-out cement mixer. We didn't own these, so their presence was surprising, but not as surprising as the idea Dad knew anything about their use. I seldom doubted my father's abilities, but that day I did. I had helped him nail fibro sheets, spackle holes in numerous walls and even handed him plumbing tape and tools when he had laid, or repaired our plumbing. But this was veering into serious construction. Literally from the ground up.

'Oh,' I said, my mind scrambling to understand. 'Have you done this before, Dad?'

'Of course!'

Wasting no time, Dad set about explaining how everything worked, while his long deft fingers used a Stanley knife to slit open the cement bags. I was fascinated by his hands—work-worn, but artistic.

'Run and get the hose, Bub.' Even though I chafed at being called 'bub' at eleven, I ran to bring the hose end to where Dad had meticulously arranged everything. I noticed a pile of sand behind the cement mixer.

'You're not making a sandpit are you, Dad? 'Cause I'm way too old for one you know, and we'd never hear the end of it from Mum. She says the only thing sandpits are good for is to provide every cat in the neighbourhood with a toilet.'

Dad rolled his eyes. 'We need the sand to mix with the cement.'

'Oh,' I said with some relief. 'Silly me.'

'You weren't to know. You never know anything you're not told.'

'So what are those long things?' I pointed to long steel rods that swirled like Mum's favourite Liquorice sticks.

'That's reo. It's short for reinforcing. If we don't use it the cement floor will sag and sink and sway.'

Dad's deep voice rumbled as he went through the details, measurements and processes. I smiled, enjoying this aspect of my father. According to Mum, Dad over-explained everything.

'Your father will use twenty words when two would do.'

When it came to the electronic devices in the house the rest of us heartily agreed with this assessment, as we were usually waiting impatiently for Dad to turn something on or tweak it.

'We could well do without all that mumbo jumbo, Max. A person just wants the blooming thing to work, not understand its 'goings on',' Mum would say.

This diatribe never worked on Dad, but each of us had begged him to 'leave off' at some time. He would just smile benignly and continue until he finished, even when we pronounced we were 'fed to back teeth' of listening to him. The more impatient we became, the more he chuckled.

'Your father's obsessed with all that 'gobbledy gook',' Mum would complain. Everyone kept silent about her own compulsions.

However, that day I was more than happy to listen to Dad's every word. After all, I'd been let out of the housework. With Mum happily inside scrubbing everything within an inch of its life, Dad and I mixed cement and laid bricks. I found there was a perfect consistency for cement—an optimum mix of sand and cement powder. Once it was mixed it was called mortar. I learned that a plumb line, which was a piece of string with a wooden weight made sure the line of bricks was straight and true. I found this part fascinating. I'd been wondering where Dad would find a ruler long enough for a garage.

Dad had already dug the ground for the foundation and had a small trench at the side to lay the bricks because the land was sloped. At least, that's how I remembered it. I know there was at least one row of bricks I laid, after carefully watching him use the trowel to smear, place and tap, then scrape the protruding mortar. The finishing touch was to wipe the bricks clean with a wet rag. When the mortar had a neat concave line between the bricks, it was time to recheck it with the plumb line.

The next Sunday there was a neat pile of timber. Dad brought his circular saw up from the work shed. This required a rather long extension cord that snaked from the lounge room window.

'You're not going to leave that blooming electric cord there for days on end, are you Max?'

'No, Else. I have no wish to die by electrocution.'

'A person doesn't need to be sarcastic, Max. Why did you have to take the screen off?'

'Didn't think you'd appreciate a hole in the flyscreen Else.'

'Humph. Certainly not!'

'Be more work for a person.'

The closing of the curtains demonstrated Mum's opinion on this further sarcasm.

Our neighbour, Guy Menzies, the builder who'd loaned Dad the cement mixer arrived about and chatted amiably.

'Got an able apprentice there Max,' he said. 'Don't think any of my four boys will be following in my footsteps even though I've got 'Menzies and Sons' in huge letters on m'truck.'

'She's good alright. Never argues.'

'Don't know enough about it to argue, Dad,' I giggled.

Guy roared laughing.

'From what I've heard, you could argue about anything, Linda,' he chortled.

'Mr Menzies, what dreadful slander!' I protested with mock affront. 'I don't argue, I debate.'

'Ha! Ha!' he responded. 'Who do you think I am? If I don't know you, nobody does.'

It was true, I spent time playing with his sons and was often in their home. I laughed.

'No,' he continued, 'my boys are all going to be bally scientists—or something. Always inventing things. The oldest is holed up in the shed doing 'electronics', whatever *that* is...' Dad also had an interest in electronics and was about to begin one of his rambling dissertations, but Mr Menzies was on a roll. 'Yeah, my shed smells of solder and David talks in another language—'diodes', 'capacitors' and God knows what else. And if my John lives to see old bones with his antics, I'll be a 'monkey's uncle'.'

Little did Dad know, the very soldering iron Mr Menzies was referring to was in fact Dad's, leased out to David by Peter, at an hourly rate. David had to come up with more money every time he wanted to work on his latest project. Our collective parents were not great believers in 'pocket money', referring to it as a 'rubbish American idea that would ruin children'. This meant any money we possessed had to be earned. The hard way—chores.

It was a wonderful day when the roller door went on the shed, officially turning it into that most coveted of neighbourhood possessions—The Garage.

'Hope you're not going to fill this with your stuff Max, and leave my car out in the rain,' said Mum.

'*Mum!*' I complained. 'Dad's done a perfect job!'

'He always does.'

'I helped.'

'So you did.'

Dad put some of his tools in the garage, neatly organised on Masonite board like the work shed, but the garage was always a garage, it never became another 'shed', in spite of Mum's fears. Whichever car we owned was never outside in all weathers.

One day Mum and I were going grocery shopping, a pleasure Dad was always happy to forgo. We were waiting for him to arrive and take the car out. He had appointed himself as the only one to drive in an out of the garage, muttering about its narrowness. This irked Mum no end. This particular day it was harder to bear, because she was in more of a hurry than usual. She rattled the keys in her hand and tapped the ground with an impatient foot.

Dad arrived and was still wiping grease off his hands.

'I don't know why you don't let me drive the jolly thing out. We've been waiting for eons,' Mum grated, looking at the keys as if considering the consequences of breaking Dad's rule.

A look of futility crossed her face. Perhaps she was remembering that whenever she'd undertaken something Dad had warned her about, things went to hell in a handbasket.

'So you've got time in your busy schedule to drive the car out of the garage, but no time to come and help with the grocery shopping,' she accused, hand on hip. She jiggled the keys, reluctant to pass them over.

'Are you listening to me, Max?'

'Of course, Else.'

'What did I say, then?'

Dad fell into an uncomfortable silence.

'See!' said Mum, triumphantly.

'Now don't get a flea in your ear, Else.'

I flinched; there were few accusations that raised Mum's ire more than this. She jabbed the key brutally into the lock.

'Softly, softly, Else. Don't go at things like a bull at a gate!'

Naturally, this offended her even more. She thrust the garage door upwards with considerable strength—with the key still in the lock. There was a clunk as the key broke. The key ring and the remaining keys fell to the ground with a thud.

'See what happens when a person is pushed beyond endurance,' Mum muttered unrepentantly.

Dad looked silently to the heavens. Would he need to drill the key out, or buy a new lock?

Cuz Buddy

Just about everybody in life wants something they don't have. You only have to watch children to know that as soon as the shine has worn of their Christmas toys, they are going to come expecting someone to listen with intense interest to their next desire.

Sometimes these desires go a bit deeper and sometimes you want another of something you already have. I already had a brother and I adored him. He was most tolerant of me. After Mum had told him to 'look after his sister' he could kindly allow me to follow him and yabber to his back. We had many fine conversations, me chattering with him grumbling about sisters. He was big and strong and protected me. When there was a snake in the bush he would stand in front of me.

'Keep still, there's a snake crossing the track. Don't move and shut up.'

He was pretty much my only companion for many years except for the cats God sent me.

I used to pray earnestly for kittens to love and keep me company. Mum probably prayed earnestly for cats to become extinct. Strangely enough, in God's upside down universe, kittens just kept coming to our house. Fluffy or tabby, tawny or black, it was all find with me.

Such was my faith in God that I would get up each morning and go to the back door, for surely there would be a kitten waiting for me. God answered prayers after all, that was what everyone told me. They had been around longer than me so who was I to question? Although there was a great reluctance on the part of grownups to actually share personal accounts where prayers had been answered I bought the Answered Prayer Promise, lock stock and barrel. So I was not amazed one morning when I went to the back door to find the cutest kitten mewing on the top step; waiting for me. I was also delighted. When I took my "answered prayer" inside to Mum she was amazed, but rather less delighted. No matter how many people Mum took on in the town and triumphed over, she turned away from forbidding this Act of God. Later, I wondered where Dad was that morning.

I loved cats; I talked to them on the back steps. They were the people missing from my life. They supplied the unconditional love and interest I so craved. I dressed them in doll's clothes, often with bonnets askew over their eyes because they wouldn't keep still. And also quite often, like the adults in my life, they just plain 'had enough of me' and went and hid somewhere.

I wanted company. I came upon the ideal solution. The lady next door adopted a little boy—I knew nothing of the facts of life and probably wasn't told anything about what adoption was or wasn't. But I woke up one morning and the grotty kid next door had the cutest little brother I had ever seen—no squalling baby but an adorable toddler. I had him on loan to play with sometimes. Soon that wasn't enough and the fertile soil of my mind came up with a better solution. I would pray for a little brother of my own. Someone like me, who would enjoy me being me, and the experience with the tot next door had shown me that little people were really good at loving you without question. A new person in the family would adore me. Naturally.

After my moderate success with God with regard to kittens, I was quietly optimistic. So I prayed for a little brother. I didn't look out the back door every morning for him the way I'd done for everything else. I was a big girl and knew that little people couldn't just sit around on cold steps waiting to be found. Just to hedge all my bets I used to throw a penny in the wishing well that was on the side of the winding dirt road that climbed the nearby Watagan Mountains.

Dad often took me on lovely mountain drives. I am not sure which one of us Mum was tired of but it was probably a double blessing for dad and me to meander around the mountains in the car. Halfway up was a wishing well. Never asking why I wanted it Dad would give me a penny to throw in the well. I would wish for a little brother. It was probably against his religious principles to donate pennies for wishing wells, but Dad could be a bit flexible, often with a knowing smile on his placid face.

This wishing and praying went on for a very long time but I knew there were lots of people for God to listen to—why there were thousands just in our church and by the sour looks on some of their faces, God well and truly had his work cut out for him.

My wish didn't come true in the way I hoped, but my mother had a younger sister, Ruth. Auntie Ruth was Mum's favourite sister, so we enjoyed many visits with them, and my cousin Chris was my constant companion at those times. We spent enchanted times together. Both curious and chatty we rambled along like two peas in a pod. This was even better than I had hoped for. We were friends. We happily designed and dug little gardens in the middle of Mum's large garden beds and earned her wrath on holidays.

We were often crouched over looking at small insects or flowers. He was the only boy I liked to play cars with because we had such fun together. I felt 'found' and accepted. I was thrilled that for those times we had each other. He had a smile that cracked open the sky. When I kneeled down to look at a bug, so did he. When I jabbered on, he jabbered back; it was bliss. Only one year younger than me he *was never* exhorted by Mum to 'look after her or else' like my older brother, but he did anyway.

His eyes would light up with interest at my nonsense and he had his own most amazing little repertoire of childhood nonsense to fascinate me. My life was complete.

My Friend Bettina

'We're planning a trick on Bettina.' The Year 4 girls in my glass gathered around me. Leticia, the ring-leader, waited for my response with narrowed eyes.

'Yeah? Really,' I said, attempting a bland expression.

I knew where this conversation was headed. Bettina Lewinsky was an outcast because of her Slavic heritage. A shy, unassuming girl with fine blonde hair she tried hard to fit in.

Bettina's mother covered her head with dark scarves and wore long flared skirts, as was the custom of her country.

She struggled with English.

Like many migrant children, Bettina had to take time off school to attend bank and medical appointments to act as interpreter for her mother. This made her struggle to keep up at school even harder. Mrs Lewinsky's eyes were bright with hope for her daughter's future in this new country.

I thought of all this as I looked from my seat to Leticia.

'Yes,' she continued. 'We're all going to pretend we're going to her birthday party and say how excited we are and all that, and then we won't turn up. There'll be no-one there.'

The others tittered around her.

I felt sick. Bettina was my friend. She lived up the street from me. I sometimes visited her home where her mother, although poor, offered spicy sugar-crusted treats. Mrs Lewinsky liked to practice her English with me and giggled shyly behind her hand when she got it wrong. I folded my arms and kicked a stone. The girls gave each other sidelong glances, ill at ease at my lack of response.

'Well. Aren't you going to say anything? Of course, you'll do it too. It won't be the same fun unless we all play along. It's just a joke. It'll be really funny. She's asked every girl in our class. It took us ages to talk her into even having a party in the first place.' Leticia flicked her long hair over a negligent shoulder. The others gathered closer to her, confident of my cooperation. Their eyes pinned me, daring me to go against the group. I remembered their barbs, their taunts. Friendship offered, then withdrawn.

'I'm going,' I said.

'You're kidding!'

'No. I never kid—not like some.' I thought of the preparations at the Lewinsky house, the decorations, the attempts at Australian food and the gift bags. 'Your parents won't like it,' I added, hoping to introduce an incentive to put a halt to their plan.

'We're not telling them, silly.'

'Do what you like, but I'm going.'

'But the party's in two weeks. We have this all planned.' Leticia panicked, her eyes were like poisonous arrows. My heart hardened. She had long bullied me.

'I'm going.'

'If you do, then you'll have no friends at all in two weeks—ever again. Think about that!'

'Why wait 'til then? Start now! What's two weeks out of the rest of my life? Anyway, I won't be losing friends.' By now they saw I was not only determined, but angry.

I went to Bettina's in my best dress, carrying a gift carefully selected with Mum who liked Mrs Lewinsky. She'd served her in the grocery shop.

I didn't tell Bettina of the other girls' plan. I felt cowardly saying nothing. When I arrived the table was set beautifully with 12 places. I handed Bettina my gift, and sat at the end of the table with aching heart as I saw the 10 carefully written named place-cards that would never be needed. After half an hour of waiting I found my voice.

'They're not coming—the others. They're not coming. They told me.'

'We will wait. Children would not do this thing,' said

Mrs Lewinsky, raising her chin. After a while she realised. Her proud eyes were cold, but only for a moment.

'Come girls. We still have a birthday to celebrate. Let us break bread together and give thanks.'

We wore hats, blew whistles, ate a sumptuous feast; then cut the cake after Bettina blew out the candles. It was her first Australian party. Mrs Lewinsky sang 'Happy Birthday' in her native tongue proudly, I sang in English, and Bettina went from one language to the other.

It was without a doubt the best party I've ever attended.

Sharing a secret

The word "holiday" at our house meant not going to school. Not for us the contemplation of exotic climes and locations. It meant chores in the middle of the day instead of just after school. Then, we began to stay at Eraring on Lake Macquarie in rented huts, or at caravan parks with other families we knew from church.

Some years later, Dad built a caravan and this heralded the excitement of the real 'going away' kind of holiday. We travelled about fifty miles to Blue Lagoon—not the island of movie fame, but a caravan park on the oceanfront. This was my first experience at the beach. I was excited beyond words. Mum wasn't. I thought this was due to her busy life, but I was to learn a secret she'd been holding close to her heart for years.

I also learned that my brother arrived on this planet with abilities that had been omitted from my genetic landscape. He had the kind of balance and athletic ability that made me wonder if he'd walked a tight rope before he had even crawled. My assessment of his sporting prowess prior to this had been solely judged on his ability to chase me around the yard. He took to the sea like a porpoise, leaving me to the rock pools. I took to the ocean like an enthusiastic, but useless sparrow—fluster and splash without progress. I couldn't swim. However, I was a resourceful little thing and decided to act like I could. Making sure I could touch the bottom of the sheltered rock pools I copied the movements of the other children. The pretence was so difficult I resigned myself to the fact I would never swim. I'd have to pretend all my life. I wondered how I'd cope when it came to water deeper than six inches.

My style was part dog-paddle, part forwards butterfly. If anyone gave strange looks at my flapping, I pretended I was waving a cheery hello. It was touch and go, but I faked it. You know you're blending in with the other kids when they ignore you, if there's an opportunity to make fun of you—they will.

After an hour of two of this awkward manoeuvring, I was shocked to realize I could no longer feel the bottom. After an initial panic it dawned on me that I was actually swimming! Although my dog-paddle style improved very little, my enjoyment level went through the roof. I didn't want to leave the water. I was a mermaid, a frolicking creature of the sea.

Until I tackled the surf. Then I was dumped with such daunting regularity my skin was red and chafed. Even my scalp stung. I would never contemplate dermabrasion as a cosmetic treatment for the rest of my life!

The sand that hadn't rubbed me raw, resided in my pants and irritated the only part left out of the scraping process on the seabed.

I gave up and went back to the rock pools. Mum sat

under a nearby tree in silent vigil. We pleaded with her to join us.

'Hate the sea,' was all she said. We thought her a poor sport indeed. I wanted to enjoy the day with her—to have her beside me in the ocean.

Late in the day when we were weary, sun-kissed and satisfied, she announced it was time to go back to the caravan. But when she tried to stand, she couldn't. I began to feel frightened.

'Have you got dead legs, Mum? From sitting on them too long? I hate getting dead legs.'

This had happened to me more times than I could count.

'Get your father—quick!' Her voice was unnatural, husky.

Dad arrived. We saw panic flit briefly across his face. With unusual speed he helped Mum struggle to her feet. Her legs were red and swollen. Half carrying her he took her to the car.

I was confused and afraid. While a friend minded us, Dad took Mum to the doctor. When she arrived back at the caravan her face was pale and her legs were still swollen and red. Her weakness and silence terrified me.

'Is Mum sunburnt Dad? How could she get sunburnt in the shade, Dad? Is she going to be alright?'

'Your Mum has sunstroke. We'll have to look after her. The doctor has given her pain relief and a cortisone injection.'

I didn't know what that was, but any kind of needle given by a doctor was bad news.

Dad set about putting her gently into their bed. Her skin was fiery red. We were shocked to see her like this. She never even got the sniffles.

'Drink up, Else,' Dad said, as he held her head so she could sip. She struggled, and then slumped back weakly. 'Go and get some straws from the kiosk, Pete.'

Peter sprang into action and arrived back with a handful of straws. Mum was able to drink small amounts. After a few hours she looked around and gestured towards the table and kitchen area.

'Do you need something, Else? Are you hungry?' Dad asked.

Mum shook her head weakly. She pointed at Peter and me. Of course. She was worrying about us instead of her own discomfort. She tried to throw one leg over the side of the bed and failed.

'Don't worry Else, I'll feed them,' said Dad. Mum rolled her eyes dramatically and Dad laughed with relief.

'Ah. You can still cast aspersions on my cooking skills, Else! Must be feeling a bit better.'

Mum grimaced in reply. Her opinion of Dad's uselessness in the kitchen was well known. Soon after we children were past toddler years, Dad had been delegated to prepare one evening meal a week to give Mum a break. He had established the menu for Saturday night as banana sandwiches and Jaffas.

'That's not a real meal, Max!' she'd protested.

To make matters worse, both of us would jump in to help him. Mum was disgusted. 'Jolly kids won't butter bread for me.'

Peter and I declared Dad's was the best meal of the week, further increasing her ire.

'Jolly father can do no wrong according to you jolly kids,' she'd moan.

She was still confined to bed in the morning, so I sat and read to her. She patted my head, smiling weakly. I wasn't sure how much she enjoyed the children's story, but I knew she was enjoying me.

'Have you always hated the beach, Mum?' I asked tentatively.

'Only since I married your father,' she said. I wondered what Dad had done to put her off the sea.

'We both got caught in a rip at the beach on our honeymoon,' she said, struggling with emotion. 'We were both raised in the country and didn't know much about the ocean. We were separated and I was beside myself with dread. I saw him go under. I didn't see him again for hours. When I came to ... your father was lying next to me on the beach. We'd both been rescued. He was vomiting up half the ocean. I'll never forget that day.' I swallowed hard.

'I grew up next door to your father in Quirindi. I realised how much I loved him after meeting shallow charming men when I left home and worked in the city for a few years. I went back to my hometown and married the boy who'd thrown clods of dirt at me over the fence. He was gentle and reliable. The best of men. We had only just started our lives together—and I nearly lost him.'

Her face was sad. I was afraid to breathe. Mum was

telling me a heart-secret. I'd never seen my tough mother vulnerable before. I waited for her to continue.

'I haven't been in water above my knees since.'

Years later Mum had to have all her remaining top teeth removed. Due to the number of extractions, the procedure was done in hospital.

My father leaned into the room where Mum was lying on the bed. She was off-her-face from the pain relief and general anaesthetic. She was drooling blood and muttering. Each time she threw a leg over the side of the bed to get up I pushed it back. I was worried what would happen if she managed to stand.

'What are you doing, Bub?' asked Dad.

'I'm putting her leg back in the bed,' I said, stating the obvious, 'she keeps trying to get up.'

Dad grinned that mischievous Irish smile and said, 'you don't have to do that.'

At eight years of age I thought **somebody** should be doing it. Enforcing bed rest for a mother who was never ill and even in her dazed state could only think of "feeding the children".

'Can ya at least give me a handkerchief, Dad? To wipe her mouth.' I said, annoyed at his seeming indifference.

Dad pointed at a box of tissues and wandered off.

I sat there for many hours, wiping the drool and blood from Mum's mouth and putting her leg back in the bed.

She improved quickly and then had to adjust to false teeth, dental adhesive and overnight denture soaking. I was horrified at the whole process. I swore I'd never eat sugar again or forget to brush my teeth.

'Why did all your teeth rot, Mum? I asked, confused about the devastation. She was meticulous with my brother and I, taking us to dental appointments every six months.

'We lived next to a sweet shop,' she said with a dramatic sigh.

Puberty panic

It was a long way home from school that afternoon. It seemed twice the distance and at the cattle grids I hopped off the bike and pushed it rather than race across full speed as I usually did. My whole body was aching and I could think of no explanation. I wondered if I was coming down with something, it was harder than usual to push those bike pedals. By the time I arrived home I was feeling worse.

The weird sensation in my lower abdomen had become heavier and I was feeling sick. I went to the toilet and froze in fear to see blood. Oh God, what was wrong? Had I hit a bump on the way home? I couldn't have. I went so slowly and carefully because I felt strange already. After a tense half an hour, I went to the toilet again and was horrified to find even more blood than before. I was really anxious then and paced the house. I must have cancer. I knew very little about any diseases, so my ability to diagnose the problem was very limited indeed, but I had heard of cancer. One thing was certain—this new thing heralded sinister news for my body.

Mum wouldn't get home until after 6 pm so I had a couple of hours to fret. I was too humiliated to ask any of the neighbour women and much too embarrassed to phone Mum at the shop. Pacing made my legs ache more, so I stuffed toilet paper in my pants, wrapped a blanket around me and rocked back and forth, disconsolate with anxiety.

Everyone arrived home at the same time and my attempts to corner Mum were thwarted at every turn.

'Mum!' I finally yelled in frustration.

Everyone was quiet. All eyes turned my way. This was new to them, I never yelled to get attention. Mum saw the fear in my eyes. She hurried Dad and my brother away, Dad to start tea and Peter to do whatever he wanted that was out of the way. With great embarrassment I showed Mum my blood-stained panties, hoping for a quick resolution. None was forthcoming. Mum burst into tears.

'Oh God! My baby is a woman!' She repeated this as if it was a great gem of wisdom, but to me it was a confusing rant.

My sensible mother had well and truly lost the plot.

After she calmed down she managed to convince me I didn't have cancer, or any other life threatening condition.

'You're menstruating,' she said, as if this explained not only my dilemma, but the entire universe.

Sadly, all it did was further convince me of her mental instability. I'd never heard the word, but it seemed to have great import to her. Ignoring my confused looks, she began to collect paraphernalia that seemed to resemble everything necessary to build a space shuttle. There was lengthy talk of plungers, inserters, pads, tampons and Meds. If the items had confused me, the words did even more so. I slumped onto the bed.

'Um,' I began awkwardly, 'Um, what are those for – and

– where do they go?' I ventured to ask at last.

'They go inside you.'

'What! Mum. No!'

Now I was really terrified. The last time we talked about things 'going inside me' was when I had the operation for appendicitis. My fear went up several notches. I eyed the items spread across the bed. None of them looked like they belonged near the human body as I understood it, much less inside, and I said so. She saw my confusion and slumped on the bed herself, lost as to how to explain this defining experience to a child with no visible body changes to herald womanhood and no knowledge of how things changed. The early onset had shocked her too.

I looked across at my Barbie doll and thought I had often wondered how I would transform into the smooth curvaceous creature that was 'the adult woman'. None of my thoughts had included anything like this!

Mum explained other changes that would happen. I would suffer great pain, become an ape, and might occasionally turn into a screeching moody cow. 'It's a beautiful thing,' she said, misty eyed. 'You're a woman now. You can have children of your own someday.' I thought of the grubby howling twins across the road. I felt a strong desire to kick Barbie, or Mum, whichever came first.

Seeing my distress, Mum sighed and pulled out some pads that would land a helicopter, and a complicated elastic belt that looked like it was designed in the Dark Ages.

'You can wear this on the outside,' she said, with a sad tear.

I rolled my eyes.

We spend ages wrangling with the suspender belt that held the pad in place. Mum patted my head softly.

'I'm sorry for getting emotional. Everything will be alright. You'll get used to it.'

'What do you mean get used to it?'

'It will be easier next month.'

'Next month! What do you mean next month? Are you telling me this horror will happen again!! Please God, no!'

Pity filled her eyes. She overlooked my swearing.

'This happens every month when you become a woman.'

'Hell!' I wished my initial diagnosis of cancer was correct. Unbelievable! A lifetime curse. I was disgusted. When I arrived at school the next day, I tentatively confided in my best friend who moaned sympathetically. Suddenly I felt normal.

'So did you go for the missiles or the landing strips?' she asked. After the display on Mum's bed I knew what she meant.

'Landing strips.'

'Good choice.'

'Do you think we will be complete screaming morons every month?' I asked, worried about this side of things.

'Darling,' she said, with a twinkling eye, 'I intend to be a complete and utter shrew.'

When I got home I kicked Barbie, packed her into her pristine plastic case and generously gave her to the little girl across the road. Let her find out the real Barbie story in her own sweet time.

No pain, no gain

Some people have either a heightened sense of pain or are tolerant to high levels of pain. My mother felt no pain.

Of course, she would have disputed this with some vehemence. The rest of us were just 'sooks'.

Our picnic day at the park near the beach at Catherine Hill Bay started out well. My mother had imbued the whole plan for the day with her usual military precision.

She was one of life's organizers. Alexander the Great would have ruled the entire continent of Eurasia if he had my mother as campaign manager. Not only ruled, but ruled over complete order and cleanliness—the usual 'Tidy Town' motto would have become 'Tidy Continent'.

The day went downhill in the car park after a leisurely picnic lunch on a tartan blanket on a grassy knoll.

Well, it had been leisurely for us, but Mum had managed to bring enough Tupperware containers filled with food for an army. This meant a great deal of preparation on her part, both before and at the picnic. Dinner at home required less work.

Dad had set her off.

'I would have been happy with a Vegemite sandwich, Else. I don't know why you go to this kind of trouble for a beach picnic.' This precipitated the Nobody Appreciates a Person speech.

'A person is never grateful for what a person does. No matter what a person does, it's just never enough.'

Of course, it didn't help that we children joined the fray.

'It's not a matter of 'never enough', Mum. It's a matter of too much,' I said, attempting to be the calm voice of reason.

'Exactly! Never happy the lot of you!' said Mum.

It was all well and good to have a fabulous three course meal outside on a blanket. There was salad, fruit cake, biscuits, peaches and custard; all prepared on the spot.

The downside to this was that the cleaning up at home later had to be seen to be believed. She never knew just how desperately we longed for a simple sandwich without fuss and bother. Fuss and bother that was the domain of the lesser mortals—we kids. We spent hours unpacking, washing up and the even more daunting chore of trying to put all six thousand pieces of Tupperware back where they supposedly belonged, in a cupboard that looked like a war zone.

It was when we were packing the picnic things back into the boot of the car when things went pear-shaped. There was something amiss that Mum's eagle eye had found, but had escaped the rest of us.

The world came to an abrupt standstill. Apparently the picnic blanket had been folded wrongly.

'How can you fold a blanket wrongly?' exclaimed my father, amazed at this new infraction of my mother's rules.

'Who knew there was only one right way to fold a blanket? Will wonders never cease?'

This treachery earned Mum's disdain.

'Sarcasm is the lowest form of wit, Max.'

Grabbing the boot bonnet she gave it a determined angry tug, pulling it onto her head with a sickening thwack. It left a deep indentation that blood began to slowly ooze from and trickle down her face.

'Oh dear, you're bleeding, Else.'

'Don't change the subject, Max!'

Kamikaze Kitty

As a child some of my best friends were cats. I loved them: strays, tabbies, Persians; cats with splotches, cats with patches, white or black paws—it was all the same to me. They never tired of the endless chatter of a small girl, never judged or told your secrets.

What they sometimes did tire of was my desire to dress them up. I put dolls dresses on them or baby clothes, complete with bonnets and bootees. When they tired of this caper they'd flee faster than lightning. Then, with bonnets dangerously askew over their eyes they crashed into the house or shed with a sickening thud. Much yowling ensued. My arrival to rescue them evinced even louder yowling, followed by a hiss or two, then I ran inside for Mum to put Dettol on the scratches on my arms and legs.

'What are you doing to those poor blasted cats, Linda?' Mum who had no liking for pets, felt sorry for my cats being forced to endure the intense coddling I gave them.

Sometimes I thought they might enjoy another of my favourite activities—spinning around until I got dizzy. Sadly, none of my moggies ever took to this pastime with relish, but would seek escape, unfortunately before they had regained their balance and collisions and yowling followed.

Kittens were the best entertainment on earth for a small girl who had bothered her brother until he was compelled to tell her to 'Nick off, will you, I'm sick of you!'

Kittens just enjoyed life and like me, they were playful. A ball of wool and a kitten will keep you more enthralled than any toy. The leaping, bounding and mid-air twisting flips were a marvel. Their ability to climb curtains or fly screens was endlessly amusing, but not to my mother.

To Mum, cats were a mystery. She failed to comprehend any purpose for cats. They were just below mosquitoes on the list of Useless Things in the Universe. My attempts to sneak them into the house did not go as well as Peter's efforts to smuggle his dog, Snoopy, inside. Snoopy would lie under Peter's bed and lick his hand in pathetic adoration; content to stay quietly in the cardboard box all night long. Sadly my cats had no such self-control, and their presence was soon evident with immediate expulsion inevitable.

'You never listen to a thing I say, do you Linda?'

'Peter gets away with it.'

'Dobber!' Peter whined, giving me the "I'll get you later" look.

'What are you talking about Linda?' Mum asked, hands on hips, eyes piercing.

'Nothin' Mum.' I chose that moment to remember my brother's ability to give superior Chinese burns.

While Dad didn't voice an opinion one way or the other on the subject of my cats, I assumed he must have a soft spot for them because he had his own pet rabbit; a huge white bunny that followed him around and jumped into his lap.

One day I had the opportunity to learn of Dad's devotion. My latest kitten had run under the house and landed in the plastic basin containing the sump oil Dad had drained from the car engine. The thick oil clung to the tiny animal and her pitiful mewling broke my heart. I sat sobbing with her in my arms.

'Put that filthy kitten down, Linda,' warned Mum.

'My kitty is in trouble and you don't care! I love her and you don't care!' I yelled between gasping sobs.

Dad came along and taking one look at the kitten, picked her up. She was even tinier with her fur slicked down, dwarfed in Dad's large hands. He took her into the laundry and filled the tub with warm soapy water. Now, as much as my kitty was distressed by the oil, she was frantic in the water in the tub as Dad's patient hands massaged the suds into her fur, time after time, to remove the oil. She spat at him, bit him and scratched him, but he calmly continued to minister to her. I sniffed and sobbed all the way through, but I knew things would be alright because my Dad could do anything. Even at that tender age, I realised Dad's devotion was more about me than his affection for felines.

It took many washes. After all the oil was washed away, he wrapped her quivering body in a towel. He defied Mum's edict to grab a rag and used one of her best towels. Then he handed her back to me. I hugged her until she was warm again and allowed me to rub her fur dry. Dad further invited Mum's ire by plonking us both down inside by the gas fire. At last she began to purr again and licked my hands in gratitude. Dad didn't fare so well. His hands were covered in scratches. Mum bathed his hands and put salve on them, then he went to the doctor for a tetanus shot. His hands were swollen for days. He shifted the container of sump oil to a shelf in the shed, far from my kitty's reach.

Kitty flourished and was more playful than her predecessors. However, she developed one alarming habit that nearly made a nervous wreck out of Mum. When she arrived at the clothes-line, after carefully negotiating the steps with a full basket of washing, Kamikaze Kitty made a flying leap at Mum's legs, claws drawn. Then Kitty executed a frisky sideways escape with her alert tail standing high, like an antenna.

Mum screamed. The basket of washing hit the ground. Half the washing had to redone. No matter how often Kitty did this trick, Mum was as shocked and unprepared as the first time. Kitty never tired of the game.

A fine romance

'When did you fall in love with Dad, Mum?' I asked one day as I stood on an orange box helping peg out the washing.

'For goodness sake, Linda. I don't know where you came from. You ask the daftest questions.'

Mum looked at me as though I'd lost my marbles. That didn't bother me at all. Most of the neighbour children told me I was nuts. They found their parents to be terminally boring. Not I. I knew they had lived a life before me and I was fascinated.

'Well, when *did you*?'

'A long time after he did,' she said.

'Oh really?' I gasped. I was on to something.

'Don't "oh really" me with your nonsense. You watch too much Disneyland. Go and bother your father.'

So I did.

'When did you fall in love with Mum, Dad?'

He smiled.

'I was fifteen.' His eyes twinkled.

'Good grief, Dad! That's a bit young. You said I couldn't go out with boys until I was 21.'

Dad laughed. A full bodied sound of joy.

'But Mum would only have been thirteen!'

'So she was,' said Dad.

This was a bit hard going, but I was making more progress than I had with Mum so I persisted.

'What did you do to show her how you felt?'

'I threw clods of dirt over the fence at her.' His face was deadpan.

'*You never did!*'

'I did.'

'But ... but ... that's awful. What did *she* do?'

'She threw them back at me, but she was a better shot.' He flinched at the memory. 'Anyway, I wasn't trying to hit her, just get her attention, but she was livid.'

I laughed. 'Livid' was one of Mum's favourite words.

'I guess you didn't do that again,' I said.

'Yes, I kept doing it. We lived next door to each other...'

'...I know that ... So what happened next?' I was hungry for more.

'We met again when we went to College. We went out for a bit.'

'What does that mean?'

'Hand me the small spanner, Bubs. Might as well help out.'

Try as I might I couldn't get any more out of him.

So I did what children have done with their parents since the beginning of time. I went back and forth from one to the other. Most children do this to gain toys or permission. There was no use doing that with my parents because they were dirt poor instead of filthy rich. This was one of Dad's favourite phrases, but it found no favour with Mum. We were *not* poor. In mum's book, we were not endowed with this world's riches. There was no use arguing for permission because to me, no meant *no*. My brother avoided this whole scenario by never asking, just nicking off. It never occurred to me to follow his lead.

'Dad said he fell in love with you when he was fifteen and you wouldn't go out with him until you went to College,' I said to Mum, hoping for more information. I climbed back on the orange box and put on my helpful face.

'I told you that!'

'But you didn't like him when you were kids...'

'Of course not. He was a gawky, stupid boy who teased me.'

'But you liked him when you went to College. Is that when you fell madly in love and married him?' I clasped my hands over my heart dramatically.

Mum rolled her eyes heavenward. 'Oh dear. I suppose you won't give up until I tell you.' There was a half-smile on her face as she settled onto the orange box beside me. I held my breath.

'We went out for a while at College. You know, to concerts, here and there. They had lots of things on. Of course we had to sit on different sides of the chapel...'

'What? Was that in the Dark Ages?'

Mum gave me a sharp look. 'Never mind,' I said, 'go on.'

'Well, I went to work in Warburton and that was that.'

'What? You mean ... you stopped liking him ... and left?'

'I didn't stop liking him. We were still friends. I just thought he wasn't for me. Didn't have enough 'go' in him.'

By the time I had another question formed, Mum was gone, leaving me gaping after her, alone on the orange box. I was deeply disappointed. I looked down at the orange box. 'Don't you laugh,' I told it, 'I'll cut you into kindling tomorrow.'

'Linda, for goodness sake! Come inside and stop talking to yourself!'

I grew tired of the instalment pace of the story, so the next time I questioned Mum was when she was brushing my hair. She did this most evenings, 100 strokes. The rhythmic, nurturing was wonderful.

'So, what happened in Warburton, Mum? Did you forget Dad?'

'We kept in touch sometimes. I met a man there. Fell hard for him.'

'Oh!' This was a twist I hadn't expected. 'Did he have enough 'go' in him?' I asked, not sure what else to say.

'Ha!' she said, 'he sure did, but it was all in the wrong direction.'

I waited.

'He invited me up to his room.'

'And that's a bad thing?'

'Certainly was, a man only wanted one thing if he asked that. It was really disrespectful. Next thing he had his hands all over me. 'I'm not that sort of girl,' I said to him. So he said that I was the sort of girl who could walk home.'

'He left you in the street?'

'Yes, just before sunset. It was dark when I got back to the boarding house we stenographers shared. I was humiliated and heartbroken. I didn't talk about it though. I'd worked hard and was working for the top boss.'

'That guy was a jerk!' I said.

'You'll get no argument from me on that score.'

'Then what?'

'After I got over that man, I realised that your father was the only one for me. He was engaged to another woman. But I had to tell him. He'd always loved me. I wanted to at least let him know how I felt.'

'What did you do?'

'I gave up my job and was transferred back near him. Then I went to him.' This narrative had me on the edge of my seat. Nothing of the story sounded like the practical, no-nonsense mother I knew. I was blown away by the risk she had taken.

'What did you say?'

'Oh nothing much. Just that I hadn't valued what I had in him. That I was his, if he wanted me.'

Dad hadn't needed any time to think. His heart's desire was granted. I didn't appreciate the strength of their love, or the true romance of their lives, but the older I became the more I realised the beauty of their love story. They threw away their pride, risked so much, gave up what they had to be together.

'Don't leave your manners at home.'

I remember my mother's reproach, that warning phrase, most usually dispensed on leaving the house, to my brother and me 'Don't leave your manners at home.' She said this after she had filched a handkerchief from my father (who always had a spare), spat on the handkerchief and rubbed real or imaginary grime from our faces. She held spit in high esteem, apart from those occasions when she witnessed men spitting in public. But when she was polishing our childish faces to bright perfection or removing a stain from a mirror or window, she would say, 'If they could bottle spit they'd make a fortune.'

After admonishing us to make sure our good manners accompanied us on whatever journey or tour, country drive or worship service, Mum would yank on her white gloves with a glint of satisfaction in her steely eyes. Dad, on the other hand, even though he had more patience than the rest of us, merely drew a straight line with his lips and calculated how long it would be before one, or the other, of his heathen children, would mess up. Who would be the first to push or shove, to cry foul, to claim malice, regret or simple boredom?

Mum would rise to the challenge on long car trips and exert herself beyond any reasonable effort to prevent warring between offspring. While holding an expanded map across the entirety of the front dashboard of the car she would simultaneously engage in "I spy with my little eye". Dad would complain that he couldn't see out of the windscreen for the flapping map then when Mum gained some control over it, he would inform her politely that it was upside down.

The truth was that Mum was the worst navigator in the history of navigation. Van Dieman would never have "discovered" Tasmania with my mother beside the helm.

Turning the map to its correct orientation inevitably led to parental consternation which had the indirect effect of stalling any animosity between my brother and I, while we waited to witness the far more entertaining scenario of our parents arguing. Parental arguments were rare and never became heated and were definitely more interesting than endless games of "I spy" or "count the number of red cars". In fact, there was a mild resemblance to Buggs Bunny and Daffy Duck.

'You missed the turn, Max?'

'Why didn't you tell me, Else?'

'I was busy getting the map out of your way.'

'Will I stop while you organise yourself?'

'Don't be silly, Max. I AM organised, it's this blasted map of yours that's misbehaving.'

'A map can't misbehave, Else.'

'This one can when you insist on having every window down for the breeze.'

'You said you were hot, Else. We don't have air-conditioning. We're not millionaires.'

My brother, curious as to the reason why we weren't millionaires, asked that question.

'Mind your own business, Peter,' said Mum and Dad in unison.

'Yes, Peter,' I said, poking him, which involved crossing into enemy territory by the dividing of the back seat into "hers" and "mine". 'Why don't you mind your business.'

Dad threatened to stop the car and 'deal with us'.

Peter poked me back.

The map tore.

Dad slumped his head onto the steering wheel.

'Why didn't you leave the thing folded, Else. I had the map folded exactly where we need to be.'

'Why didn't you tell me that, Max.'

'I always fold the map Else.'

'Are we lost?' I asked.

'If a person is going to criticise a person for everything a person does then a person should just take over.' Mum proceeded to fold the map awkwardly.

'Don't just fold the thing any old way, Elsie. I'll never get it back to where it was.'

Mum shoved the map into the glove box.

'How far to the next town, Else?'

'How would I know Max. Apparently I can't read a map to save my life.'

'I'm thirsty.'

'He poked me.'

'She's on my side.'

Toe to Toe

Early in life Mum and I had parried over a million subjects.

Dad's assessment was that neither of us knew when to leave well enough alone. He was, of course, right.

I began as a toddler with questions: 'Why can't my cat talk?' 'Does God wear pyjamas?' 'Who's in charge of all the money in the world?'

When I was five I walked into the kitchen while Mum was mopping the floor. This activity involved vigorous swishing that left streaks of water up the wall and was accompanied by loud thumping as the mop hit whatever was in the way, occasionally a miscellaneous child.

'Get off my clean floor, Linda!' she yelled. 'How many times do I have to tell you blasted kids.'

'But you're on it,' I said, facing certain disaster. 'And your feet are bigger than mine. Why do you walk over the floor while you're mopping it anyway? If you started at the other end you'd finish in the laundry without walking over it.'

'Look at you, all of five, telling me what to do.' She snorted and gave me The Look—I'd seen her use it on Dad often; the "You're A Right Smart Arse" look.

When I was older my opinions confounded her as much

as my earlier questions. I developed anti-royalist sentiments that confused her. She revered the monarchy. We sang *God Save the Queen* at every function, local, church or school.

I told her God was not in favour of the monarchical system. I read a text from the Bible where God gave in to the Israelites and let them have a King like the heathens so they would learn what a ridiculous idea the whole royalty gig was.

She was appalled. The only thing worse than a smart arse was one with God on their side.

Christmas Rescued

Our parents were heroes. All of our holidays involved road trips. Having been a parent for some years, I find myself in awe of their commitment to travel so often with two children. There was never a question of alternate modes of transport, these being beyond our means. Why, air travel was for celebrities, captains of industry, or politicians. All of whom were in a different world to us.

We planned to visit Mum's sister, Monnie, and her family in Bathurst. Auntie Monnie worked on a peach orchard. Our visits usually coincided with the prime of the yellow peach season, but this year we were going to share Christmas. This meant travelling down to Sydney and then up to Bathurst. Our cousins confused us by saying we had to go 'up' to Sydney and then up to Bathurst. Never one to hold my tongue, I argued that anyone with a map knew Sydney was below Cooranbong. Dad spread the map of on the table and gave 'the willing' (only me) a lengthy and enlightened explanation of the journey. After this I confidently offered to navigate.

Mum snorted. 'Really, Max. The kid doesn't know up from down.'

'Are you going to be navigator then, Mum?' I questioned.

'Ha!' was her only response. This did not bode well, but we soon learned Mum and Dad had taken the trip so many times a map wasn't necessary at all. Mum forbore making that point because family equilibrium was essential. After all, we'd be in the car for many hours.

Every car trip needs only to start with an argument to set the tone of the journey. And two children with endless hours confined in a car have an astonishing ability to find numerous reasons for dissent.

'She won't sit still!'

'Dad, he's on my side of the seat!' (Yes, we'd drawn a line!)

'Tell her to be quiet, Mum!'

'He's digging me with his elbow again.'

Mum courageously entered into a gazillion games of 'I spy', another travelling quirk I forgo whenever possible.

Despite Mum's best efforts we children continued to quarrel, incurring parental wrath. Dad had offered to stop the car and 'deal with us' when things took a turn for the worse. The radiator boiled not long after starting the long climb up the Blue Mountains. With steam pouring out from under the bonnet, Dad sighed and pulled to the side of the road. Ironic really, when Dad had been threatening regularly to 'stop the car'. This irony was lost on us when we realised just what a boiling radiator entailed. We sat by the road in the mid-December heat, swatting at flies and complaining about the dust.

Dad always carried a large container of water. They didn't call him 'belt and braces' at the factory workshop for no good reason. Filling the radiator was a speedy solution and greeted with fulsome gratitude by all. We returned to the car where Peter and I continued World War III with some enthusiasm. Unlike us, Dad was silent throughout the episode because he knew a boiling radiator doesn't know when to let up.

This scenario was repeated all the way to Katoomba. We inched up the highway, stopping to look for water—sometimes in the bush. This worrying repetition took the edge off our holiday anticipation, and also quelled the commitment Peter and I had to fight with each other. We were silenced by the greater tyranny of the prospect of being stranded. Only one reproof was necessary when we claimed to be 'dying of thirst'. After a lengthy wait at a garage at the top of the mountain for the radiator to be repaired, we were on our way again. I made the wise choice to sit as far as possible from Peter.

Worse was to come. When we arrived at Auntie Monnie's place, we found there had been a misunderstanding. She already had a houseful of people. It was decided we would stay nearby in a local boarding house/hostel. This seemed like an adventure—until we arrived. The hostel was crawling with enough insect life for David Attenborough to do a whole series of documentaries. Mum's eyes widened as soon as she entered the room. We knew that look. Spiders, ants and all other insects were not permitted to walk on our paths, much less enter our abode.

'Good grief,' she said, taking great care not to touch any of the furniture or walls.

Dad was struggling up the stairs with our luggage. He knew that look too, so without uttering a word he turned and started back down again.

'Oh Max, we've come this far. It's family. It's Christmas. Just take me to the nearest store and I'll get some Gumption.'

Mum scrubbed that room until it glowed. We climbed wearily into our beds. We slept soundly until midnight when we were awakened by Mum's screams. Sleepy-eyed, we sat bolt upright. My brother, who'd fought to have the top bunk, fell noisily to the floor. There stood Mum with one of her shoes, surveying the squashed corpse of a cockroach she claimed was 'the biggest ever created.' Dad climbed out of bed and started to get dressed.

'Not now Max,' Mum said. 'We'll last 'til morning.' Our Bathurst Christmas was over. After banging noisily on the landlady's door, Mum treated the woman to a pointed diatribe that included Mum's favourite maxim '"cleanliness is next to Godliness". 'You should be grateful not to be reported to the authorities. And you would do well not to expect any monetary gain, now or ever,' Mum informed her with steely eyes.

Deeply disappointed, we travelled home. I cried and Peter sniffed, although quietly. Our parents had been through enough. We expected to forego Christmas, or at least part of it, but no Christmas would ever be cancelled on Mum's watch. The next hour took on a magical Mary Poppins feel. Dad had a tree up in no time. Mum threw the Christmas decorations around the room as if there was no tomorrow. Nothing was left undone. The gifts were hastily arranged willy-nilly around the tree. Lemonade and cake were put out for Santa and Rudolph.

'What about Prancer and Dancer?' I asked, rushing in where angels feared to tread.

'I'm not after feeding every reindeer on earth!' said Mum, in a voice that brooked no argument, and carried the vernacular of her Irish ancestors.

What could possibly go wrong?

'What are you blooming kids doing up that tree?'

The booming voice of our neighbour caught the attention of John and me. We were ensconced in the highest tree in Hough's backyard. Hough's lived next door to our house and across the road from John's. Earlier that morning we had come up with the brilliant idea of making and using a parachute.

I think we might have watched a television show the night before and been inspired. Reasoning it couldn't be too hard, we'd "borrowed" one of my mother's sheets. It had been conveniently hanging on the clothesline.

Then we'd taken a roll of nylon rope from Dad's shed. We hadn't bothered to ask about that either, after all we'd return it all quickly. No one would ever have to know.

Predictably, once we had scaled the tree (no mean feat in itself) the shine began to fade on our 'brilliant idea'. Simply put—reality set in.

However, we were reluctant to admit our stupidity. John and I shared the philosophy of having a go at a good many things that had our parents 'tearing their hair out'. And this day we'd outdone ourselves. Naturally, our common sense had kicked in. Neither of us was going to launch ourselves out of the tree, so we came up with several circular conversations to delay the inevitable moment of coming to our senses and abandoning the idea.

'You go first John,' I muttered, looking down. The distance to the ground seemed greater with each passing minute.

'You go. Ladies ... er ... girls first,' said John gallantly.

So it was a huge relief when the neighbour yelled up at us. 'Get down here this minute ya stupid galahs!' he shouted.

It may have been the first time in our short history that we obeyed instantly.

In the Fifties and Sixties we made our own fun. Parents were not inclined to provide or assist in our various entertainments. They gave us the very strong impression that they did not want to hear certain things from us; whining on any subject, excuses about homework, pangs of hunger—even if they verged on starvation status, requests for treats—this included anything other than water from the tap. 'You've got arms and legs. What are you bothering me for? Can't you kids see I'm busy?'

Another thing we'd rather die than admit to, was boredom.

That particular complaint inspired parents to write lists of chores that would keep us busy until we were adults and left home.

Parental lectures incorporated the oft repeated lament: 'I don't know what's the matter with you kids. All you want to do is play, play, play. Bloody easy life you have. Why, in my day, all we did was chores, chores and more chores.'

This was just the beginning of lengthy monologues on How Hard Life was When I was a Kid. The list was endless, ending with a totally blighted life history, where they'd suffered the equivalent of child slavery, with the added curse of poverty. Explanations and speeches of this kind were to be avoided at all costs. So all conversation on the subject of What Can We Do? was entered into with our small playmates. Now, the sad factor of relying on advice and feedback from this quarter was that our friends were universally short on common sense. Those of us who posed the question, 'Whadya reckon we could do for fun?' were really only looking for someone to agree that our latest hare-brained scheme was inspired. When it was, at the very least a truly bad idea, or at worst, downright dangerous.

The day was a scorcher. The tree-house was in dire need of repairs but this meant applying to parents for timber, assistance or advice. None of which would be forthcoming. Our attempts to obtain a swimming pool had been thwarted by an inconsiderate parent, a neighbour, who'd made the generous offer that if we dug the hole, he'd supply the rest.

Too easy, we thought—until we put our shoulders to the task, our muscles to the spades and discovered that not only had we grossly underestimated our abilities, we had in fact afforded all the parents a great deal of entertainment by our naivety. Ha bloody ha.

We vowed it would be a century or two before we believed another word from adults, or asked another question of them.

'Whatdya reckon. . .' began John thoughtfully.

It was a promising beginning, but misleading, because John, like me, was impulsive and the opposite of cautious. Together we concocted the worst endeavours known to mankind.

'Yeah?' I asked, feigning indifference. But after a few hours of frustrating listlessness I was ready to listen to anything.

'Whatdya reckon would happen if we swung around on the clothesline?'

'Sounds like fun to me.'

'Yeah, but what could go wrong?'

'Well, nuthin really. Our parents are all at the meeting in the hall for another two hours.'

'Yeah, they wouldn't catch us and the tattletale kid next door is down with chicken pox, so he won't see and rat on us.'

'If nuthin can go wrong, why do they tell us not to do it?'

'Beats me. Always ready to spoil a kid's fun, parents are.'

'Yeah, they just want us to suffer like they did.'

'Too right, all that rubbish about walking to school carrying books that weighed a ton.'

'With shoes with cardboard lining because of holes.'

'And only eating bread and dripping for years.'

'What's 'drippin'?'

'Dunno. Some stuff everyone ate when they were depressed or somethin' like that.'

By now, our conversation had become as boring as the

day and after a few more languid sighs, the temptation proved too much.

Our combined brainpower had not come up with any consequences, so we leapt up and caught an arm each of the clothesline.

We decided it was best to choose opposite arms to balance each other. Because the clothesline was closer to the ground near the path at the back of the house, we were able to get a bit of speed up by running when we there, which made the clothesline spin faster. We were airborne and filled the air with squeals of delight.

Even in my faded memory, it was the best fun I'd had in years. The sensation of flying through the air, shrieking in joyous abandon was unparalleled for sheer exhilaration.

After what seemed ages, we tired and threw ourselves on the grass, sated with pleasure. I lay on my stomach, watching the ants marching through the grass.

'Geez Linda, take a geezer at that!'

I turned to follow John's gaze. My stomach fell straight through to my feet. In that moment, I knew what it would feel like to fall several hundred floors in a plummeting lift. While two of the arms of the clothesline pointed straight and true, the other two competed to reach the ground. Curved downwards like disappointed branches.

They spelled doom—ours.

Our frantic attempts to straighten them were fruitless. We discussed the contents of our fathers' sheds. All our postulations regarding crowbars and levers died on our drooping lips. Our lives were over. We might as well emigrate. Write our own adoption papers.

Even though I had a well-rehearsed line in begging for mercy and a repertoire of grovelling apologies, I knew it would be courting disaster to even trot them out.

I was not even to be granted solidarity as my delinquent partner in crime took off home because he feared my mother more than his. He remembered my mum hit harder than his and didn't mind punishing "guests", whereas his mother only walloped her own offspring.

The secret life of my father

I couldn't believe my ears.

The jubilant sounds of honky tonk music filled the house. It wasn't the telly. I went to check our piano. There was my father, who I had never even seen sit at a piano, playing with gusto. He looked up. Along with the usual twinkle, there was a slight wariness in his eyes. 'Don't tell your mother.'

I nodded, pleased to be part of his conspiracy. If Mum knew he could play the piano, there would be no end to the nagging and pleading for him to play in public. There would be words of 'duty and wasted talent'. The likely thrust of her arguments would be to push Dad in the direction of playing in church. Dad's shy nature would shrink from the glare of the spotlight. Why, he only ever stood at the front of the church to adjust the sound system, or occasionally went to the microphone to say, 'Testing, one, two, three.' He seemed uncomfortable even doing that.

I zipped my fingers across my lips. His secret was safe.

'Good girl.'

'Play some more, please Dad,' I begged. 'Just for me?'

Dad lost himself in the joyous rhythms of honky tonk music, the soulful sounds of the blues and then swung effortlessly into the famous hymn, 'Abide with Me'.

'Wow! How can you play without sheet music, Dad?' I asked in bewilderment. This was confusing. I'd been studying the piano for a several years, fingers struggling laboriously over every note.

I was always curved anxiously over the piano, looking from page to keyboard, note for note, then back again, never quite connecting the two. And there sat Dad, playing as if music was his mother tongue, working the piano pedals effortlessly, as his hands glided over the keys. Dad answered my question about the lack of sheet music with a vague statement about playing by ear. He made it look so easy. I knew of his passion for Broadway musicals. Every Sunday would find the two of us happily ensconced in front of the TV for the midday movie. We watched Gene Kelly, Fred Astaire and Ginger Rodgers, Jeanette MacDonald and Nelson Eddy, Frank Sinatra—pretty much any musical on offer.

'How come Mum doesn't know you can play like that? Weren't you at College together?'

'Oh, your mother doesn't have to know everything. I never played the piano at College.'

'How long have you been able to play like this?'

'Ages, I guess.'

I gave up prying and just let me music lift me, up and away. Then, suddenly it was over.

'Ah, duty calls,' said Dad, closing the piano lid and springing from the piano stool, leaving me in a land of magic, hungry for more.

These special times were infrequent and random, but they never coincided with Mum's presence. Dad made a Hawaiian guitar, he played it quite often at home for us all. Mum didn't pressure him about playing this in public, deeming it 'unsuitable for church', but she made no secret of her pride in him, 'Your father can do anything.'

For myself, I wished I could play something—anything. After four struggling years, even Mum had to agree my musical talent was non-existent. But she persisted with my brother, buying him a cornet. Mum believed in giving her children Every Opportunity.

'Oh Mum! Couldn't you buy Peter something quieter?' I moaned whenever he practised. In my opinion his musical ability matched mine—he had none. 'Buy him a flute, Mum. They're really quiet.'

'Stop picking on your brother, Linda. He'll get better with practise.'

He didn't, although he must have improved his breathing capacity, because he got louder.

'Your father doesn't have to know everything,' said Mum as we sat quietly in her blue Mini Minor outside our house.

Mum and I had just indulged in our shared passion—buying fabric. Max and Clare Roberts were friends of my parents and they owned a beautiful fabric store. This was a place I dreamed about at night. I learned to sew quite early in life. It provided me with the freedom to design and make my own clothing as well as a creative outlet. I no longer had to endure wearing navy shirt-dresses that Mum declared made me look slim and elegant. It was my opinion they made me look like I was in the Navy.

'We better go in I guess,' I muttered, looking down at our pile of fabric bolts, all neatly wrapped in brown paper. There were yards and yards. We really had over-indulged. Mum sighed. I knew she was thinking the same thing. Her mind was ticking over. 'Go and see where your father is. Then come and tell me.'

I was more than happy to comply. Most of the fabric was for me, because Mum still hadn't moved on from the one dress she'd made me when she went to 'Tech'. I knew what was expected of me. With the stealth of a spy I slipped into the house. When I knew Dad was well and truly busy in the shed, whistling while he worked, I ran out the front door and beckoned furiously to Mum. She leapt out of the car. I stayed 'lookout' while she stacked the fabric bolts into the wardrobe in the spare room.

This chicanery was also repeated on other occasions when Mum bought dresses or shoes for herself. It was a great piece of farce as Mum had her own money and so did Dad. Thus, there was more pretence than actual deception going on. Once when I was on lookout, Dad sauntered past and winked at me. I flushed bright red until I realised he was enjoying the game. I thought it was really funny after that. They both had secrets that were pretty tame.

'Why don't you just tell Dad when you buy clothes, Mum? He wouldn't mind.'

Mum paused, a cloud crossing her face. Maybe she was remembering her lectures to Dad on the 'exorbitant' cost of his tools. 'Ah, he doesn't need to know.'

'But what about when you come out in a new dress? What then? He'd have to know then!'

'Nonsense! Your father wouldn't notice if I was wearing a hessian sack.'

Mum nearly jumped out of her skin early one morning on our way to church, when Dad blithely commented on how lovely she looked. 'That's no hessian sack, Else,' he said, with a wicked grin.

'Hummph,' muttered Mum, frustrated at being caught out.

Dad, however, was never caught out. I later learned that while he was a student he played honky tonk music for the dances at the community hall on the 'wrong side of the tracks'. I found a photo of him in elegant flares, posing like a professional, with a three piece suit and carefully arranged tie pin. He stood confidently; hand on hip, casually leaning on some nearby railing, looking very sharp indeed. His eyes were full of whimsy and intelligence. There was no sign of the reticent, retiring man I knew as the public image of my father.

So much for shy.

They shot my Daddy with a gun!

I woke early on November 23, 1963. It was my ninth birthday. I had to wait until my tenth birthday for my first real birthday party, but I was still excited because Mum had made me a Dolly Varden cake.

This is a fruit cake made in a pudding bowl. A doll is placed in the cake, so when it's iced it appears to be a beautiful doll with a flowing dress. Mum had iced my cake with the palest pink fondant and piped a white lace edging around the hem. My doll wore a lace hat and was adorned with blue ribbons.

I yawned and headed towards the kitchen.

Crash!

There were the sounds of smashed glass and a shocked moan. Oh no, not my cake. I ran to the kitchen. Mum rushed past me—face white, eyes wide. My cake forgotten with the dramatic turn of events, I followed her into the lounge room. She was staring aghast at the television. My eyes turned to the screen. I heard the word 'assassinated'. An image flashed of a handsome man and an elegant woman, smiling from an open top car. I knew this man. He had a smile that lit up the sky and a deep firm voice. I always held my breath a little when he spoke. Mum was a self-confessed news addict. I had often seen John Fitzgerald Kennedy on the evening news. I knew he had a daughter about my age, and a cute little boy who was always holding his daddy's hand. 'There's a man who'll stand for the right though the heavens fall.' I'd heard Mum say.

Being a child of endless curiosity I'd watched and listened. I loved his voice. A voice that was unafraid, unapologetic and ringing with conviction. I thought him wonderful, looking beyond his stirring speeches to his fatherhood.

I ran outside and vomited, until exhausted from dry retching, I lay on the grass. What sort of a world was it when men killed good men? When fathers were gunned down in the street? I was dizzy with disbelief. I was surprised that the

Australian November sun shone with its usual relentless glow. Birds still sang. My chest hurt. I loved him the way one does a childhood hero. He had the courage to say words other men didn't want to hear, and would not fall silent. He made decisions and then stood his ground, not faltering or rambling like many other leaders. I'd watched them too. I hated the world that turned on John Fitzgerald Kennedy and killed him on my birthday. It was November 22 in the United States of America, but it was my birthday in Australia on the other side of the world. The nation mourned with me, his nation, mine and many others. I didn't touch my birthday cake, even though Mum begged me to 'at least try it.'

'Give it to the little girl without a Daddy. I hate America. They should change their name to the Useless States of America,' I wept to Mum. 'How can a country kill its own leader?' I ranted. 'Are they barbarians? Do they all have guns over there? We don't even know anyone with a gun. How can they be civilised when they're worse than heathens? What did they kill him for? They voted for him!'

Mum patted my head, enduring my ravings as she would not have done on any other day. 'The world has gone mad,' she agreed sadly. 'But you're too young to think about these things.'

'How can I not think about it? He has a daughter my age. She had a father yesterday and now he's gone.'

'You can't grieve for the whole world, Linda,' Mum said with quiet resignation.

She knew this would not be the end of it for me. I

thought of all the games of 'cops and robbers' and 'cowboys and Indians' we kids played. I thought about our game rules that decreed if you were 'shot dead' you had to count to ten before you were allowed to 'get up' again. I vowed never to play those games again. John Fitzgerald Kennedy would not be getting up again. Dad scooped me up and took me outside to the shed, giving me an important job he couldn't do by himself.

'Will someone shoot you with a gun, Daddy?' I sniffed, unable to be diverted so easily. 'I couldn't live without you.'

Dad sat down and drew me onto his knee.

'They shot President Kennedy because when a man leads a country, madmen want to silence good men.'

'But you're a good man, Daddy,' I responded. I was not reassured.

Dad sighed. 'It's different. When a man is as important as a President, the more great things he says, the more people want to be his enemy. Some crazy man wanted him to be silent.'

I pondered this.

'You're not very important, are you Daddy? … to other people, I mean.'

Dad smiled. 'No darling, I'm not at all important.'

'You are to me,' I said, throwing my arms around his neck. 'You don't say great things to people, do you Daddy?' By now Dad's smile had widened and his eyes were twinkling.

'I make a habit of never saying a single great thing to a mortal living soul,' he said, hand over heart.

'You're never going to be President are you?'

Dad roared with laughter.

'That's okay then.'

A few days later, while we were driving into town, the car windscreen shattered with a loud bang and fell onto Mum and Dad in the front seat. With a scalding rush of tears I threw myself onto the floor sobbing and screaming.

'They've killed my Daddy! They've killed my Daddy! The Useless States of America have shot my Daddy with a gun!'

'Who the blazes...'

'Who the blazes are you?' Mum's voice rang through the house.

Silence.

This was odd. Was there an intruder?

'Who the heck do you think you are coming in here?'

I walked through the house in the direction of Mum's voice.

When I arrived in the lounge room I was as gobsmacked as Mum.

There were two strangers, sitting on separate lounge chairs. One was a middle-aged woman, the other a long-haired youth. The woman put her hand over her mouth and shook her head. Her lack of speech was compensated by the other stranger.

'Ar were shurphhin an ah wahf shhmsht dow...' the man said, then made a grunting noise of frustration. 'Yar shhee, mishers, sh'arrd decshplarn, arr I wantsch ter...'

This was too much for Mum. 'Get out! Get out of my house!'

The woman screamed.

Mum went for her apron strings. This was a habit of hers at the first sign of trouble and she carried it out in a manner that was reminiscent of the gunslingers of old. No one took an apron off like my mother. If she had been a Head of State, the removal of her apron would have signified a declaration of war. I wasn't surprised the woman had screamed. I often felt like it when I was the cause of the apron coming off. It meant action.

The man opened his mouth wide and pointed inside.

'*Shoo!*' said Mum.

The woman grabbed her bag and ran out, leaving the screen door swinging.

'Shut the door properly!' yelled Mum, 'honestly, some people! Born in a tent.'

The young man saw this as an opportunity to offer greater explanation. Sadly, it was as incoherent as his first attempt.

'Pfft. Drug addict.'

'Blooming intruders. What's wrong with people?'

At the word intruder the young man's face took on a startled look.

Mum advanced on him. 'Are you deaf or stupid? I said *get out!*'

With one last confused look the man bolted. Also leaving the screen door banging.

'No care for a person's property,' said Mum, clicking the door shut herself.

She turned to me. 'What do you make of that, Linda?'

'No idea, Mum.'

'It's not like you to be short on ideas.'

'Beats me.'

'Hmmph.'

Silence.

'It's a mystery,' said Mum. 'Who were they?'

I shrugged. 'What did they want? On a Sunday morning?'

'Couldn't understand the hooligan with the long hair and the woman had nothing to say for herself.'

'I wonder if they were together?'

'Didn't seem to be. That dopey bloke seemed to be on drugs.'

'Wonder where they are now,' I said.

'Hmmph. I might go take a look,' said Mum. She walked outside and I followed. We looked up and down the street.

'No sign of them.'

'Hope it doesn't happen again,' I said.

'Doesn't bear thinking about.'

A week passed.

'Who are you blooming people?' I heard Mum's voice.

I skittered from the kitchen around the corner to the loungeroom. Mum was standing with her hands on her hips, scowling. There were another two strangers sitting in our lounge chairs. They took off faster than the previous two. The mystery had deepened. Mum and I put our heads together again and came up with nothing.

'What gets into complete strangers to decide to make themselves at home in a person's living room?' asked Mum.

Dad's opinion was sought.

'What did they say?' he asked.

'Nothing,' said Mum.

'Didn't get a chance,' I added. This impertinence earned me a sharp look from Mum.

'I think one of them was on drugs,' said Mum. 'A muglair young bloke with long stringy white hair.'

'Very descriptive, Else.' Dad grinned.

Mum folded her arms. 'Just trying to be helpful, Max.'

'Did he say anything?'

'He tried to,' said Mum, 'but all that came out was nonsense. He wasn't the least bit coherent. Couldn't understand a word.'

'Did he look like he wanted to cause trouble?' asked Dad.

'No.'

'Hmm,' said Dad, clearly as perplexed as Mum and me.

'The fool opened his mouth wide. Not a tooth in his head,' said Mum.

'Oh, why didn't you say so, Else. They are probably looking for the dental technician's house. Our place looks just like Eager's.' Dad smiled.

Tommy Eager lived a few doors down and made dentures. How simple.

'Mystery solved,' I said. 'Why didn't we think of that, Mum?'

'We're not as smart as your father, that's why.'

'Our place *does* look the same, Dad... Hey, Mum – maybe we could change the front porch so people don't mistake it.'

'I'm not shifting anything around to suit complete strangers who can't find their way out of a paper bag,' she said. With a thoughtful look on her face, Mum took her apron off. This time, it was one of those 'you don't wear aprons outside' actions.

'Oh, dear. Where's she going, Dad?'

'Ah, you know your mother, Bub, she's probably going to talk to Tommy Eager.'

'Oh dear. He's a good friend of yours, isn't he?'

'Was,' said Dad, then seeing my panicked face, added, 'Just kidding, Bub.'

On Mum's return we learned that the long-haired guy had been surfing and lost both dentures. The woman had come for a fitting of her top denture plate. Mum had stayed for a 'nice chat' with Tommy and was happy to have the mystery solved.

A banana

'If you eat half my banana I'll eat the other half,' I said to the lunch monitor, who was the Headmaster; a bristling autocrat with a short fuse. This wasn't a lunchtime school swap arrangement.

Our bags were regularly searched. After being corralled in the shelter shed to eat our lunches the duty teacher would check our lunchboxes to see if we had eaten everything. Some teachers omitted this tyranny, but Mr D did not. Carefully positioning himself at the exit point and effectively cutting off access to the rubbish bin, there he stood, like an eagle-eyed Napolean assessing enemy agents. If all but a few crumbs remained in wax-paper wrappers, inmates were permitted to throw their papers in the bin.

Our school bags, often old suitcases, were left where the sun's harsh rays could wreak havoc on the most carefully prepared lunch. There has never been a sandwich that benefited from being lukewarm. Our mothers were never aware of this because being a tittle tat was punished at home and abroad. So we got used to warm lunches and silence. My mother, having survived poverty, the Great Depression and flour-bag underpants, set a generous table and applied the same to our school lunches.

The banana was just shy of being "on the turn" at 7am in the morning, by midday it had definitely turned.

I opened my lunchbox for inspection. The existence of an uneaten banana incensed the teacher.

'What's this Brooks?'

I spoke slowly. 'It's a banana, sir. Or it was this morning.'

'Don't give cheek, Brooks. You're skating on thin ice.' With the item identified, Mr D stabbed a short finger at the fruit.'

'Why haven't you eaten it, Brooks?'

The sight of the blackened skin would have enlightened even a myopic man, or perhaps a better man. And even though I hated stating the obvious I always gave him the respect of an answer. Silence is not my jam.

'It's rotten. It has gone off. Sir.'

This set him off. 'There's nothing wrong with it, Brooks … blah blah …' those starving children in Africa, the perils of bad nutrition…He saw me eyeing the rubbish bin and his face grew red. He would not be thwarted by a child, and this particular child had gotten under his skin on more than one occasion.

'Eat it, Brooks.' he jabbed the words at me. 'You're not leaving here until you eat that banana.'

'Our bags, student bags, are left in the sun, in the area specified in THE RULES, sir,' I said, thinking of the fridge in his office. The office where several canes were hung from the walls in medieval warning to wayward miscreants. 'Things go off in the heat, sir.'

I hoped my repetitious use of the term "sir" annoyed him as much as his penchant for only ever addressing me by my surname. He had never spoken my first name in my four years of primary school.

'If you eat half, sir, I'll eat the other half.' I picked the banana up delicately and held it up to him.

'GET OUT!'

I am trouble

It is a wonder I learned anything in primary school because I was so often sent outside for distracting others. I had been caned a few times and didn't fear the canings of the teachers. This shocked the boys I was lined up with outside the Principal's Office for 'The Cane'.

Sometimes our class teacher caned us, and sometimes we were sent to the Headmaster. One day there were a few of us in the queue. We got talking and compared the tally. I was shocked to realise I'd actually been caned more times than any of the boys.

Being a religious school they also offered the 'complete repentance package'. After the caning, you were taken to a small room to pray and confess your guilt to God and show true humility, committing to never repeat the crime. This was a very inauspicious room that was actually the teachers' coat-room.

There among the coats, lunches and wet umbrellas you went with the teacher you had offended and knelt down to offer your repentance to God, who must surely be equally offended.

One of the girls in my class was caught stealing drinking straws and told the teachers I'd taken some too. Stunned, I tried to defend myself. 'Straws!! Good grief, I didn't even know you had any? We don't even have a kiosk. If I took them why didn't you find any on me? Or with my things? Yet you found hundreds of the things stuffed down the front of her dress, but not mine?'

However, this was insufficient to plead my case without reasonable doubt, so we were both caned. Then it was off to the coat-room. She went first, her lying face wet with tears. It was then my turn.

I pled very eloquently for God to impress the truth upon the teachers and expressed fervent sorrow for their mistake in not believing my innocence, followed by the sincere wish for them not to do it again.

I was never taken there again. The other kids asked me why. 'Ah, teachers! Who can figure them out?' I shrugged.

I came under the firm and unflinching hand of Mr D in the classroom in Year 5. He was a short, hard-muscled man. My brother referred to him as, 'built like a brick shithouse'. He reminded me of Yosemite Sam, the cartoon tyrant.

Mr D decided to treat my garrulous conversations as a declaration of war. Not many days would pass without him sending me out of the classroom, telling me where to stand, and how.

'Stop skipping on the way out, Brooks!'

'Oh, sorry sir.'

It wouldn't be long before he realised I was providing a show for my classmates who were peeking out the window and tittering. Then it was, 'Further Brooks, further.'

On one occasion he repeated this until I ended up on the nearby high school grounds. When it was time to come back in he yelled out, 'Get back here, Brooks! And some straight here!'

Pretending I couldn't hear him I cupped my hands up to my ears and waved my arms helplessly. He called again. I repeated the action and shrugged. He came closer. He called again.

I kept up the charade until he was standing in front of me. What is wrong with you, Brooks? Couldn't you hear me?'

'No, sir. I didn't want to disobey and come back without permission.'

His face reddened. 'Get back in the class. You've missed recess. I hope this has been a lesson to you. Go straight to the room. *Do not deviate! Do you understand me? Can you hear me now, Brooks?'*

I detoured through the playground, jumping over the swings on the way. I didn't look back.

He would be the calm voice of reason until he warmed to his subject, or until one of us lesser mortals incurred his wrath. He seemed to find my questions confronting. After an exuberant class discussion Mr D pronounced he was exasperated with my arguing.

'Why is it was 'a discussion' when you give your opinion and 'an argument' when I give mine?' I reasoned.

'You, young lady are on detention for arguing. You will stay in at lunchtime and write 'I must not argue with the teacher 100 times' on the blackboard.

So I did—

> I must not argue with the teacher 100 times, once or twice maybe, but not 100 times.

In primary school I often played cricket with the boys. Mr D, the athletic school principal, sometimes played with us. He also taught Grade 5 and 6. I admired him a great deal, so when I learned I would be in his class for my final primary school years I was excited.

However, I soon learned that he controlled with humiliation and caning.

In the steel equipment cupboard at the front of the classroom was a big pointy dunce hat. I was appalled. Children were made to wear it, stand in the corner and face the wall. They shook, there were sounds of distress—sniffing or sobbing. Occasionally, a child wet their pants. I was incensed by the inhumanity. I wanted him to target me. I'd be ready. Then …

'Brooks! Come up the front!'

The door to the steel cupboard squeaked open. The dunce hat came out. With fire in his eyes, Mr D held it toward me with an outstretched, determined arm. I wasn't going to waste the opportunity.

I collapsed on the floor, laughing hysterically. I worried that I'd overdone it, but nervous titters and snorts from my classmates reassured me that I had them on my side.

There wasn't a whisper in the room.

I stood up, dusted my uniform, and smiled. 'I'm sorry, sir, but don't you think you could put the dunce hat to better use by giving it to someone who will actually be humiliated, instead of the one who got 95% in Maths this morning?' I paused. He was red-faced and raging. I knew I was courting a new kind of trouble but I had to try and break the power of the DUNCE hat.

Quietly and submissively I put my hand out to accept it. 'It's all right. Give it to me. Five minutes or ten?' I asked, and when he didn't respond I said, 'Ok, 15 minutes.'

With a quick snap he put the hat back in the cupboard. 'Get out, Brooks!'

'Yes sir. How far this time, sir?'

The kids surrounded me at recess. 'What were you trying to prove, Brooksie?'

'You have to accept the punishment, but you don't have

to accept the humiliation. My uncle served as a stretcher bearer in the war and he says they can take your life but no one can't take your dignity.'

The dunce hat didn't make another appearance. However, the retribution I feared arrived a week later. Swift and terrible. After some minor infraction I was taken to his office for 'six of the best'. Apparently in some dark corner of the world it had been decided that six was the maximum number of times a child could be hit with the cane. It was the first time I was given all six cuts. He was livid.

I howled in pain after the first ferocious sting. He wasn't holding back.

'What's wrong with you, Linda?' asked Mum when I arrived home. 'Why are you pulling your sleeves down? And why in heaven's name are you wearing a jumper on a hot day like this?'

Silent, hot tears streamed down my cheeks. I had feared this moment – when my mother would find out how much trouble I was in at school with Mr D.

I turned my red, burning hands over. I looked at the floor. Any hope that I could hide my shame quickly died. Reluctantly, I lifted my hands. They were clawed and covered in angry blood blisters from wrist to fingertip.

'Who did this to you?'

'Mr D.'

'Right!' Mum tugged at the strings on her apron and flung it on the chair. My heart thudded. She fetched her hat and coat. I began to tremble. Without explanation, Mum placed her hand under my arm. Thrusting the house key into her coat pocket she started up the street. I wondered where we were going, but was afraid to ask.

After what must have been nearly a mile we walked down a laneway between houses and Mum thumped a large brass door knocker. The sound thundered through the house.

A smiling Mr D opened the door. Oh, no! I wanted to die.

'Ah, Mrs Brooks, what can I ...?'

'Don't Mrs Brooks me!' she said, voice as cold as ice. She lifted my hands and turned them over. I kept my eyes on the ground. 'I only want to know one thing ... What does any child ever do to deserve this? Don't answer! There is nothing you hear me. Nothing.'

'I cane her brother all the time...' Mr D blustered, clearly discomforted.

'She's a little girl.'

Mr D opened his mouth, but Mum's upheld hand halted the words. 'Did I give you the impression that I came here for a conversation? Linda didn't deserve this – she's never any trouble at home. Anyway, that's beside the point – I don't care what she did. This ... this is unacceptable...' Her voice held cold fury. Mr D had no response, but Mum wasn't finished. 'I could have you. I could have you in so many ways your head will spin. I could have your job, your livelihood, your career. Do you understand me? I can make your life hell. Do not mistake me in this. And, I will be keeping her home for a week. The little dot can't even feed herself, much less hold a pencil. Do not expect a doctor's certificate. We all know how that will go. I will be at the school tomorrow to get work for her to do at home – she will be disappointed to miss school. You should be ashamed. My daughter will never be caned again. By you or anyone. Do you hear me?' Mum spoke slowly and clearly.

I raised my eyes, stunned by her words. Mum wasn't prone to long speeches. With her, brevity was an art form.

Mr D was as white as a sheet. 'I ... I ...'

'I don't want to hear from you,' said Mum, slamming the door in his face.

Again cradling my arm, Mum turned. We walked back home. Mum didn't say anything to me. She didn't have to. I looked up at her as she strode homewards. My hands stung, but my heart soared. My mother was on my side in life, utterly and completely. I was convinced that there was no other parent who'd do what she did. And with such style. She was a lioness.

Mum's outrage did not die out. She retold the story over and over, often punctuated with, 'they're only kids, we all got into mischief'. After my initial anxiety had worn off and my hands had healed I began to enjoy the telling.

'Did you muck up at school, Mum?' I asked in astonishment.

'We had a Miss Horrabin at our school,' she said.

I giggled.

'Of course, we called her Miss Horrible.'

'Was she horrible, Mum?'

'She certainly was – she whacked us over the knuckles with the steel ruler for crossing out a word. Horrible, alright. We never said it to her face, of course. But one day...'

I was on the edge of my seat.

'...one day I drew a picture of her in the back of my notebook and wrote Miss Horrible next to it.'

'OH!'

'She saw me scribbling and came and grabbed the book. She was as mad as a cut snake.'

'Oh, no! Did you get the cuts, too?'

'She called me to the front of the room and had the bamboo cane ready. Then my brother Cliff ran up and broke it in half while he yelled at her 'don't hit my sister'. Then he threw it out the door and ran home.'

'Oh my, what did your mother say?'

'She never knew. I suppose Miss Horr... er... bin must have forgotten to tell her, and Cliff wandered around and didn't go home until the right time. I loved him for that – he was my hero. No one touched me when he was there.'

Child Whisperer

After returning to school a week later Mr D was no longer the Headmaster. I had been transferred to the "Rural Room" Kindergarten through to Year 6. Nothing was said about my caning. I could only guess what had gone on behind the scenes. It was unheard of for students to transfer to another class mid-year.

As usual, I started chatting to classmates when I finished my work.

'Outside Linda. We need to have a talk.'

I put up the usual defences, so I wouldn't cry when I received the obligatory caning that I expected.

'Do you know why I'm punishing you?' she asked.

'I was talking.'

'Well, yes and no. I'm punishing you because I love you.'

Tears ran unchecked down my face. I couldn't believe what I had heard. I didn't hear that at home. Her warmth touched me profoundly.

'When you talk to the other kids you're stopping them from learning, from getting their work done.'

'But why aren't they finished too?'

'You are brighter than them, BUT that comes with responsibility. They need more time. And you're interrupting them.'

I was ashamed, understanding the consequences for the first time.

There was no caning. Miss Schowe told me that she saw in me the woman, the person, I could become. She told me what a great kid I was, that I was gifted, that I had potential, but my behaviour would stop me from becoming all I could be. She told me I needed to learn quietness and stillness. She understood that I was bored. She would give me more work. She gave me two first graders to care for whenever I finished my work. I was being rewarded and trusted. My heart swelled. I had been given two little people. They were mine to help. Judy and Julie. I couldn't get to them soon enough to sit with them and listen to them read help them do their sums.

I became her willing slave. There were no more crimes, no more punishments. I was never sent out of the room. I was no longer Brooks, I was Linda. From Miss Schowe I learned the difference between humility and humiliation, self-worth and self-importance. For more than a year I was privileged to sit at the feet of a truly gifted, gentle teacher, who for me at the tender age of eleven, changed my heart, my life and my purpose. The best teachers we ever have are those who not only care, but compel us to raise the bar for ourselves—call us higher than we imagine; who introduce us to our possibilities and give us the keys to our future. Those who not only teach us how to succeed in the world, but how to 'be' in the world.

Linda Brooks

Years after leaving school I searched for Miss Schowe for 40 years through every avenue. I finally received her email address, and gave her my grateful thanks in the words I expressed above. She replied swiftly—

Dear Linda,

What an amazing surprise to get your email, and what a touching affirmation of a life's work, thank you so much for putting it on paper for me!!!!!

It is what we hope for every day when we teach, but we are so hampered by our humanity and personal foibles that we fall short so often. There is no way of knowing whether we have made any difference at all until someone takes the time to tell you. I have had many notes and expressions of thanks over the years but yours so captured the essence of my teacher heart more than any other has ever done, that it brought me to tears.

I will keep it and treasure it as long as I live. Linda, thank you for taking the trouble to track me down; you made my day!!!!! Irma

I met with her and was able to tell her all that had been in my heart. Time rolled back as we exchanged photos and filled in the years. She was just as I had remembered. If anything, there was a sense of fun I hadn't been aware of as a child.

A Sporting Chance

To sport, or not to sport. If you want my opinion, which is dubious indeed, the answer is NOT.

As kids at home we spent a lot of our time outside. This suited Mum because our presence inside meant dirt on her pristine floors, crumbs on bench-tops, and pillow fights that were often instigated by Dad and generally a 'load of Tommy rot'. So outside we went.

I discovered Sport when I went to school. I was originally excited about it. After all, I'd been very active before arriving through the doors of my educational future. At my first Sports Day in Grade One I actually came first in one or two running races. I didn't embarrass myself in the other events, thus avoided ruining my short life. Then something mystical happened. My classmates grew taller and I didn't. At first I didn't notice, but Sports Day came around again. No matter how much effort I put into running my showing can only be described as poor. Not so lowly as being last and sobbing all day, but pretty close.

It was time for the sack race. I'd seen the previous efforts of the other kids. Knowing my speed wouldn't get me far I resorted to technique. While everyone else hopped like crazy, I put my toes firmly in the corner of the sack, yanked it up between my legs and ran like hell. I even had time to look around at the end to see everyone else halfway up the field. Fabulous you say? Maybe then, but try telling an audience of adults at any gathering years later the only sport you were spectacular at in school was the 'sack race'!!

Things got worse as the years went by. Even my horse-riding attempts invariably ended in the dust. At school, the only reason I wasn't picked last was because I could be counted on to debate any given point or rule with the teachers, even if I didn't have a clue what I was talking about. Very useful when in need of extra time, but not much else. I spent my time quite happily in the outfield.

Pam McBride put us on the basketball court to form teams and called out my name.

I was aghast. 'You're kidding me! They're giants! What do you expect me to do? Run between their legs?'

I got out of it. Probably because the other kids complained I was a downright nuisance and "forgot" the rules.

Iris Yob put me on the hockey team. Ye gods, who invented that sport—le Marquis de Sade? Making matter worse, we didn't have protective gear, but apparently I was needed for the numbers. Iris was sure all I needed was a little encouragement so she persevered where others had given up. After all, many of the other girls were petite.

So Miss Yob worked harder with me, but she didn't realise my instinct for self-preservation outweighed my competitiveness; basically I had none. Who really cared? Well, pretty much everyone else as it turned out. I became so bad that when I saw June Muldrock barrelling towards me, I gave an elegant bow, graciously waving her to help herself to the ball. I was sidelined. Ah the relief.

I loved the water, so some hope was held out for me there. But the requirement of breathing while moving through water eluded me. I was again relegated to the stands. This was a real nuisance on Inter-School Sports Carnivals, when the non-competing students, were only allowed to cool down in the pool for a few minutes in the intervals.

This ineptitude didn't ruin my social standing as much I thought it would. Perhaps I seemed more human when the other kids found that my compulsive attitude was confined to the classroom. Outside of it, I was just another kid 'mucking up' at every chance.

The fettler

Every family has a raconteur, a storyteller. An aunt or perhaps a grandfather would could gather and spin a tale that held, enchanted and entertained.

My paternal grandmother, Anna Brooks, was our family storyteller. Between cousins and friends there was no dispute that she could weave an ordinary day, and imbue it with magic. One often hears of a person universally loved and we wonder if time has erased their faults. But Nana Brooks deserved the description, and no-one loved her as much as her grandchildren.

She had a favourite knee rug. It was mohair and tickly, pale lemon-and-brown check. Her name was sewn in the corner. It was soft and fluffy. I would tuck Nana into a lounge chair and sit at her feet, in much the same way as her many grandchildren, who were proud to share her. There was plenty of Nana to go around. Though poor all her life, she loved with extravagant grace, and believed with unshakeable faith.

She was unique.

I awaited her visits with a hungry heart, racing through her chores, applying a thoroughness that was usually lacking, looking forward to the time when Nana would be mine alone. Running with the mohair blanket, and tucking it firmly around Nana, I would sit on the floor. Even on the warmest of summer days Nana allowed this awkward tenderness.

'Which story would you like to hear?' she asked, her warm dulcet voice already weaving its spell.

'The one about the man who fell from the roof when he was shingling and broke his leg, then had to be taken to the doctor in a bumpy sulky, behind a black horse with a shimmering mane.'

'Oh, Linda,' laughed Nana. 'You've nearly told the story yourself. What is left for me to tell?'

'Oh lots! Lots, lots more.'

So Nana would tell it again and again. I never tired of any of her stories. They were always surprising and funny.

Her eyes would mist over when I invariably asked, 'Tell me about my grandfather.'

'His name was Charles. He was a very dapper gentleman.'

'What's 'dapper'?'

'Smartly dressed. He always wore a vest with his suit, and his tiepin was perfectly placed.'

'Was that why you fell in love with him?'

'Oh no. He was a gentle man, kind and true. Not all gentlemen of fine birth and breeding are gentle.'

'Oh.'

'And he always smelt wonderful.'

I giggled. 'Did he wear aftershave like Daddy?'

'Well, I didn't know the secret for a long time.' Nana paused. I's eyes were wide. 'Oh, do go on.'

'He used to keep a sprig of lavender in his suit pocket.'

'Oh, that's wonderful. I hope I meet a wonderful man who carries flowers in his pocket.' I sighed. 'Tell me about when you got a job on the railroad.'

Nana O'Day laughed. 'It wasn't exactly on the railroad. It began like this... I went for an interview... 'Oh, my...' the rail inspector said when I walked in dressed in coat and gloves, 'we're not accustomed to having women apply for positions as fettlers.'

'The inspector looked me up and down. He was nonplussed. It wasn't as if the position called for great strength, but it did require making sure the rail gates were open on time – come what may. Women tended to be involved with child-rearing alone back then. It was uncommon for a woman to work outside the home, much less with a 'man's job'. Many women took in laundry and cleaned for the wealthier homes in town.

'Clearing his throat, the man viewed we prospective employees. Quite a few had turned out, all of them men apart from me. He had to have someone employed by the end of the day. He smiled. There were nearly 30 in the community hall. He must have thought it wouldn't do any harm for me to sit the test along with the men.

'I was so quiet and polite with my hands folded in my lap, hoping that he couldn't bring himself to turn me away. Your Grandfather was very sick and I needed income for the family. Leaning into a large box the man took out dozens of balls of string. The task required each person to unroll the ball of string and then rewind it by hand. Patience and focus was crucial to the position – an unopened gate could cost a rail disaster, and left open it would cause chaos with wandering cattle.

'There was no written test as some of the best men couldn't read or write other than sign their names. One by one the men left in various states of frustration. I was the only one who completed the task. With small children at home and a sick husband, I was delighted to become a fettler for the New South Wales State Rail.'

.

Shingle Splitters Summers

'Good grief, Dad. That looks like a whale skeleton,' I said.

'You've got an imagination there Bub, I'll give you that.' Dad continued to plane the curved boards with rhythmic precision, clearly enjoying my confusion. 'How's the surface going on that frame, Pete?'

My brother ran a practised hand over the timber. 'Feels pretty smooth, Dad.'

'Good, son.'

There was a load of washing to put on the line, but as usual Dad's projects held greater appeal than any form of domesticity. 'Can I…?'

'You'd be a help if you tied Snoopy up somewhere else, Sis,' said Peter.

'Aww, leave off! He's too strong for me. He runs round in circles, winds the chain around my legs and pulls me over.' I eyed Snoopy with reluctance, and received his usual tongue lolling grin and thumping tail greeting. 'Anyway, where'll I put him? There's only the clothesline and I have to hang the washing out.'

Peter rolled his eyes. Dad looked up, and pointed to the back step where Mum stood, hands on hips. 'Washing won't hang itself, Linda,' she said.

'Doing it, Mum.'

'You're a heck of a long way from the clothesline and basket for someone who's "doing it", Linda,' she said.

I ran to the clothesbasket, threw it in the trolley and lowered the line.

'Forget anything Linda?' asked Mum.

'Aaaah, I don't think so…'

Mum held out the peg basket.

'Oh. Right.'

'You'd forget your head if it wasn't screwed on,' said Mum. 'Leave the men alone.'

Mum smiled at "the men" with pride. Not for her the nagging of weary wifedom over half-completed projects strewn across backyards for years. Dad finished what he started. If Mum ever complained he was taking too long at anything we kids started a uproar 'Fair go, Mum. You've gotta be kidding!'

We holidayed at Eraring with an assortment of other families. Years earlier we'd gone on travelling holidays in the little round caravan Dad built, but lately we'd been renting cabins on Lake Macquarie.

We often spent Sundays at Shingle Splitters, a point that jutted into the saltwater lake dividing it into a calm haven on one side and a windswept reedy curve on the other. Sometimes the wind turned, its mercurial gusts rampaging both sides, or the calm one - the side that sloped gently into the salt water lake.

Cobalt-green water crimped in midday breezes as it lapped with metronomic lyric on creamy sand. Tall pines extended to the end of the point. A hilly area where eucalypts, pines and scrub gathered indifferently allowed children a secret domain, where shrieks of 'You're it, tagged ya' echoed over the water.

Then it all changed. The speedboats came with their growling engines, pristine fibreglass perfection, water thumping speeds, mile-wide wakes and spitting spray. They heralded a new kind of weekender—water skiers. We moaned that our peace was ruined, our favourite place had "gone to the dogs". Even Mum ceased her crossword puzzling in the shade of a tree to squint at the newcomers and mutter 'Hmmph.'

Dad got an inscrutable glint in his eye. He and Peter took off on trips to the marina at Toronto.

'Crikey, Max,' said Mum, 'you're not looking at those fancy expensive boats are you? In our dreams.'

However, come summer, we were the proud owners of a sleek speed boat with a gutsy roar, and dashing blue strip Dad had meticulously painted. It spewed smoke with the best of them. So we learned to ski - and by that I mean Peter morphed into James Bond, while I survived as long as the boat went in straight lines, which didn't happen much. There I went, careening off at a perfect tangent to the trajectory of the boat, where I sank in ignominy and had to be pulled aboard spluttering, with my life jacket choking me.

Freedom comes

In spite of being in trouble, school gave me my first real sense of achievement and pride. Here was a place where I could succeed. I had a place to find answers, freedom to think my own thoughts. I remember my excitement on first discovering school. It was a new world—an Aladdin's cave.

At first my good grades didn't sink in to Mum as meaning much. She probably expected it was a passing phase. Perhaps she thought the teachers were merely being polite when they referred to me as 'a delight' and 'sharp as a tack'. At the end of primary school Mum accepted I was a star at school. Her delight and pride knew no bounds. She had given birth to a straight A student. The Universe in its wisdom and kindness allowed me a brief shining moment in the sunshine of my mother's adoration.

God smiled. Fate chuckled. By accident Mum had produced a child hungry for knowledge; impatient for life with a mind like quicksilver, and just by accident she loved me for it. I set out to enjoy every moment I was the sun in my mother's narrow solar system. Her praise fell on dry thirsty ground and was soaked up immediately. Everyone else tired of her commenting, 'Linda's the dux of the school, you know.'

She no longer required me to conquer domesticity; after all, I was clever, so she accepted a lesser standard. The struggle to include me in the endless round of household rituals took second place to making time for me to do my homework. The constant need to advise and instruct didn't cease. I wasn't a princess. I still had chores, but she left my bedroom alone at least, turning it from a battleground into a haven. It also began a time when school became my domain. At least there my decisions were unquestioned.

Dad had come to realise in my contented hours with him in the shed that I committed none of the crimes attributed to me by Mum and he refused to mete out any further beltings. When I began to menstruate he made one simple statement that meant my freedom from the fear of physical reprisal.

'No-one will ever hit my daughter again.'

I remember his steely eyes, his soft words and quiet determination. Then, he looked at me and sorrow and forgiveness passed silently between us. It was a new day in our relationship, treasured and never forgotten.

As long as I live and no matter what argument is put forward, no matter what creed espoused, no matter what 'holy edict' is thrust to the fore, I will never understand how causing a child to fear physical pain or separation from parental love can ever achieve anything other than a hungry childhood—sending into the world a young person who perceives love as unpredictable. One who believes you must work with every fibre of your being to be good enough to be loved.

I would love with a hungry heart.

With school shining a favourable light on me, Mum had finally found common ground with me—my success. She would sit quietly for hours, listening with tired satisfaction to me read my assignments out loud to her, brushing my hair while I read. This was a precious measure of affection. She was working longer hours so I took on the evening meal preparation and she cleaned up after tea, happy to allow me to study. With the pressure lessened, weekends were more relaxed. Church days meant friends and guests were welcomed for meals—lavish spreads of food. It was time to think of her children's future marriage prospects. Our home became a social hub.

Dad and I continued to watch the Sunday musicals. Although Mum sighed over this 'waste of time' she didn't interfere. Life took on a new rhythm. Suddenly in her eyes my future was full of possibility and opportunity. I would not be a failure; therefore she would not be a failed parent. Maybe she glimpsed a world of learning she could not possess or conquer; a world of difficulty she could not face or master. Maybe she just wanted to sit at my feet, admire and love me.

School also gave me my first taste of freedom. It opened the door to another world and at fifteen I vowed to be the master of my own destiny. My life was still dictated by strict religious practices, rules and constant criticism from Mum although my time with Dad continued to be peaceful and uncomplicated.

I yearned with a longing that made my chest ache for the

day when I could leave home and find a place to belong. I knew I would never live a confident life unless I did. I would choose a career that gave me instant financial independence and somewhere to live. Then I would live on my own terms and make a home of my own. I never spoke of the secret longings of my heart, everyone expected me to pursue the heights of academic success. Because Mum espoused no rights of teenage privacy, although I loved to write, I never kept a diary.

I held my dreams close to my heart, all I ever wanted was a home and family to lavish with love.

A new fish bowl

'What are you doin' here kid? Shouldn't you be in Kindergarten somewhere?' The voice came from a tall, robust boy. It was my first week at high school. Now, *everyone* towered over me.

'I didn't realise there was a test for size,' I responded. 'Silly me, I thought all I had to do was pass exams.'

The boy chuckled and called to a mate. 'Will ya look at this one! Only comes upta m'knee and has a mouth on it!'

'Well, pardon me for not being a deaf mute,' I said.

They roared laughing. 'You can be our mascot,' said the tall boy.

This set the tone for my new life at high school. I had been worried about being teased and taunted. I'd heard of dreadful things like dunking of heads in toilets and other tricks played on unsuspecting kids, but after a while I realised that most of the nonsense was carried out by the boys on each other.

There were new freedoms. The library was open all hours. And the books! Such a selection. I was soon engrossed in tales of Greek mythology, books on art and ancient history. Then there were the literary classics, Dickens, Austen, T S Elliot. A whole new world had opened up to me and I couldn't wait to learn. This curiosity was viewed by my classmates with indifference or eye-rolling. To my surprise, my new teachers were not offended by my quest for knowledge even if it meant endless questioning. Suddenly that was what school was all about.

It was the beginning of forming relationships with teachers based on mutual respect. I joined the debate team, often switching sides at the last minute when someone failed to show up. On the whole, discussion and opinions were recognised and rewarded.

In the early days we were lined up in the quadrangle that also served as the bat tennis' court, and given the new rules.

'What's new about them,' I muttered, 'they're just the old rules warmed up like leftovers.'

'Quiet, Brooks!' boomed a voice.

I shrugged. Not everything had changed in this brave new world. Rules were still "suggestions". I ran around barefoot. This annoyed the hell out of the teachers. When they approached me about it I expressed deep gratitude to them for caring about this. I professed to be greatly distressed as 'those damn boys, sorry Sir' had thrown my shoes out of the window again, and I was relieved they'd noticed and would now help me find them. 'I don't have time for this nonsense,' was the usual reply, and I'd scamper off—shoes safely in my bag.

I once confused Mr Solomon so much with my blah blah, when he came upon me truanting with my best friend Kaye, that he gave us a lift in his car to the shops. I sat jabbering in the front, politely enquiring about the health of his family, while Kaye sat in the back speechless and frozen in fear.

In Year 8, I came upon a group of older boys struggling to climb the flagpole and replace the flag with a tea towel.

'You're all useless,' I said.

'Oh, hoh! As if you could do it!'

So I did. The boys cheered. I bowed. The teachers came. They assembled the whole school. They dug in deep for a long wait and the usual silence. The inquisition began. It was over quickly. When they asked, 'All right, who did it, speak up? We're not leaving until the culprit confesses' I owned up readily. They looked at me, this tiny girl, in disgust and gave me a speech on the ultimate fate of liars. They pronounced the boys cowards for hiding behind the skirts of a girl.

'How'd you do it, Brooks?' a teacher asked quietly later.

'Simple physics, Sir. Smallest monkey climbs the highest tree.'

There are people in life I probably should have taken pity on, but didn't. Predictably one of these people was a teacher. Even more surprising, she was one of my favourite teachers. After all, Miss Pam McBride had given me private elocution lessons during late primary school and I had enjoyed them. I had enjoyed Miss McBride immensely. Sadly, the elocution lessons were not as successful as I'd hoped.

I was reunited with Miss McBride in high school. And dear Miss McBride found the focused 'one-on-one Linda' was a whole different ball game to the Linda in a class of 25 or so. It's not that I meant to be different, it just happened. I got bored when I finished my work. While this wasn't a problem in our solo sessions, Miss McBride soon found this propensity disturbing while trying to manage a couple of dozen other kids. And try she did, anyone who knew Pam knew that.

'The Rules' seemed to serve a greater purpose for the teachers than the students. This was completely undemocratic. Miss McBride wasn't the only one who found my attitude confronting. Our principal, Mr Ernst, also found me provoking.

Mr Ernst was not fond of the curriculum. The reason for this was because he didn't choose it. Every English class began with, 'We have to study this for the curriculum, but....' Mr Ernst and The Curriculum were at odds with each other. Never was this more evident than when we studied the famous literary work, 'Animal Farm'. However, Mr Ernst was a conscientious man who favoured his students achieving well over failing. His reputation rested on our precarious success. So he gave his all. But the struggle with his conscience was clear. I remember upsetting him during one English class when he asked who the reigning pigs represented in the book and I replied, 'Teachers.'

Mr Ernst was fond of giving long and laborious impromptu lectures in the Principal's Office, for students suffering from wayward thinking, but for reasons I could never fathom, he never chose this option with me. Even as I saw the temptation to take me aside and explain the evils of communism sweep across his face, I knew he would resist the urge.

On the whole Miss McBride and I travelled along well. However, several times she decided to 'take me to task'. She 'took', but I didn't arrive.

The first time occurred when the school bell had sounded to summon us to class after lunch. A rather animated discussion with Athol Grosse had delayed me, and in order to arrive in class on time, I broke the rule of 'never go through the middle classrooms'. I chose the first doorway. It was the Art Room—Miss McBride's sacred domain. By the time she apprehended me I was in the middle of the crowded corridor, surrounded by the general crush of students. Now Miss McBride felt she should be on the same page as the other teachers, and hand out a little corporal punishment. But she didn't have the stomach for it. So she would get the blackboard ruler and give us a perfunctory 'paddle on the backside' as a token effort at discipline. This particular day she grabbed the first thing that came to hand. It was the six foot long art ruler.

'Stand still Linda!' she said, denouncing my crime, eventually getting to the punishment part. My eyes were as round as saucers and this greatly impeded her ability to give me an effective 'ticking off'. She'd already lost steam when she said, 'Turn around you little Miss!'

'You're kidding me! That thing's a mile long! If you swing that out here, you'll end up hitting twelve kids and be sued by at least half their parents,' I said in an awestruck voice. 'AND you'll probably miss me!'

'Oh get on with you,' she muttered, her shoulders slumping.

'Please Miss McBride. I'm late for class now. Will you write me a late note?'

'Oh for goodness sake, Linda. Know when to leave well enough alone!'

'Yes, Miss.'

The next occasion was completely accidental. I swear. And totally not my fault, I must say. I was hungry and Miss McBride was teaching long past class time. Although we were never allowed to be late or leave early, this didn't apply to Miss McBride—she was often both. So I began to eat my sandwiches at the back of the classroom. I only hid this activity because of the goodness of my heart—I didn't want to hurt her feelings. It certainly wasn't to avoid trouble; although this was exactly what I was constantly accused of doing. All was going well until Miss McBride asked me to say grace. Normally only too happy to perform this task—a mouthful of Nutolene and bread didn't permit me to say a word. Now, anyone who has eaten Nutolene knows exactly where this is going. There is nothing on earth you can do to make Nutolene disappear down your throat with any speed.

Miss McBride was taken aback at my silence. She knew she could always count on me to make a supplication to the Lord on any given occasion. Even if it meant I 'occasionally' slid my latest protest or cause into the prayer, it was better than asking one of the kids who refused point blank. Her eyes filled with disappointment. My eyes filled with tears. I couldn't chew. She'd see me. I couldn't swallow. I began to wish I'd put a bit more tomato sauce in the sandwich. A sandwich I could imagine becoming lodged in my throat if it stayed there too long and dried out. I shook my head in what I thought was a soulful manner, desperately hoping she would think I was either depressed or ill. But I had no history of either condition so she remained perplexed. By now everyone was looking at me. This was usually enough to have the most hardened student embarrassed, but I was feeling really bad for letting her down. With sad resignation, she said the prayer herself and watched me take off at lightning speed. She didn't see me spluttering in the hall. Of course, the rest of the school did.

Later in the year we went on a beach walk for our mid-year class picnic. Miss McBride was our class teacher. Sitting around the bonfire as evening fell, she attempted to touch our blossoming souls with a heartfelt talk.

'Kill it,' I screamed. Miss McBride slapped me.

'Not me!' I bellowed, 'the spider!'

I pointed in terror at a huge huntsman that had decided to join our group and was mincing menacingly towards us. One of the boys felt the call to masculine duty and began to chase it. After much screaming, (from the girls) and hilarity, (from the boys) the spider was duly dispatched, and we sat back down.

'You!' screeched Miss McBride, pointing at me, 'You're incorrigible! You've spoilt the mood.'

How that was down to me, and not a huge hairy spider, was beyond me. I said so. My thoughts on the subject were not appreciated.

The following peace lasted for many months.

Miss McBride often arrived late. This was not remarked upon. We sometimes arrived late. This was on a par with committing a 'war crime', and her scalding rebuke took up the remaining class time. One day she picked on one of the kids who was trying to look after a sick parent as well as attend school. I'd had enough of this double standard. A few of those who knew me well saw a glint in my eye, but I shook my head. We would live to fight another day.

The next time Miss McBride was late I quickly organised the class into two halves. One half was to remain while the other half went and hid. Because she had the alarming habit of looking frantically for anyone who was late or out of class too long, I knew my ploy would work. While Miss McBride was out looking for the first group, the second group went and hid...and so on. I impressed on the kids that in order for the plan to be successful, they had to be on their best behaviour, when returning, and in class, keeping their heads down working like they never had before.

I remained in my seat the whole time, coordinating operations. For the next two hours, Miss McBride searched for half the kids, returned with them to find the other half had gone, and so it went. Left half missing. Right half missing. With Miss Innocence Brooks totally absorbed in her schoolwork and surprisingly oblivious to the 'goings on' of her classmates. At the end of the double period, Miss McBride was exhausted. There was no class that day. No one learned anything.

Then again, Miss McBride was never late again.

First job

My first job was at a roadside vegetable stall. I was twelve. I rode there on my bike, weighed fruit and vegetables and was shouted at by the crabby woman who grew the vegetables. I once got the price wrong and had two bob taken out of my pay. My mother was a grocery store manager, but it was quite obvious I had inherited none of her talent.

After high school, and before nurse training at the San, I worked at the SHF. The place was never the same after that. Not only was I slow off the mark, I wrecked things. I started in some steamy room packing Vegelinks into tins. I could never fit the right number in and no matter how I tried the last one was always torn and squished and had to be thrown out. After a few days of this malarkey I was thrown out, although they were kind enough to call it a 'transfer'. I was put on the Weetbix machine. As the women deftly picked up 6 in each hand and place them precisely in the boxes, I picked six up in each hand and broke the outside ones – four broken out of twelve was not considered acceptable.

I was moved to the cornflakes line. There were twelve women, six to a line. They were not impressed with inexperienced staff fresh from school, so they gave no advice or assistance but sat there scowling or gossiping about their sex lives – all this with a beady eye on me, waiting to giggle at my discomfort. I pretended to be deaf, which didn't bother them much when they were yakking, but annoyed the hell out of them when they wanted to tell me what to do. Six jobs a side, 1. Catch the cornflakes out of the shute into a plastic bag and place on conveyer belt, 2, 3, & 4 are a bit hazy, 5 someone rolled down the plastic bag. 6. someone put the toy in.

I managed the toy insertion quite well, but it was on the catch cornflakes that I really stuffed up. I only managed to catch 2 out of 3 on a good day. I didn't have many good days. When you missed the cornflakes they landed in a bin at your feet. With my imprecise muddling the bin to be emptied often, which meant both lines shut down.

Now while the women showed no interest in efficiency and speed to deliver more than necessary they were appalled at my ineptitude. I told the foreman I couldn't keep up with the machine and he sped it up. Greaaat! Now I was catching one in four. I watched how he sped it up a few times and when he was gone I opened the hatch and slowed it down. The women gasped, but I caught every single one then.

However, the machine, and thus all 12 women were forced to speeds that embarrass a snail. They murmured and complained in suitable Biblical fashion so I hummed a very slow waltz. Out of tune. The foreman would return and speed it up. I would slow it down. It broke. They sent an electrician.

My brother. 'It was you, wasn't it Sis,' he declared as he set about fixing the machine. It took half an hour. I pretended to have a power nap.

As soon as he left I started again. The foreman was suspicious, but for some strange reason none of the women told him. He looked at me through narrowed eyes when the thing shut down the second time.

'He'll go and tell the big bosses,' warned the women.

'Rubbish,' I said, 'you don't really think he's going to go over to the office and say a teenager worked out how to do his job?'

I was transferred to a far corner of the factory where all that was required of me was to pick the skins off peanuts as they went along a conveyer belt. The peanuts had already been tumbled so there wasn't much skin left. It was here that I discovered an unusual phenomenon. Much like sitting a train the train next to you is moving, it was hard to tell just what was moving and what wasn't.

A friend came and watched me. I was mesmerised. 'Hey, Brooks, you're not getting many skins there. Those peanuts are rushing past and you're missing them.'

'Oh,' I said, 'the peanuts aren't moving – the machine is. If you watch it long enough that's what happens.'

She laughed and walked off.

However my school nemesis was on the prowl, she'd been working there two years and full of self-importance. My ineptitude was her opportunity.

'Jeez, Brooks. Not the dux of the school here are ya? You're completely useless.'

'I know,' I said, 'isn't it marvellous. I'm getting the same pay as you and I'm absolutely rubbish at everything.

Accidental feminist & part-time tyrant

I'd skived school and was weighing potatoes in the STAFF ONLY packing and loading area of THE TRADING & CO-OPERATIVE STORE, known colloquially as THE CO-OP.

I made tedious work of this task, choosing potatoes of varying size, putting them on and off the scales, attempting exactness, until Mum asked what the blazes I was doing, then said. 'Just make sure you're over. Always. Never jip people.'

Mum stood at the back of the store eyes narrowed, hand on hips. After a thoughtful *Hmmph,* that portended trouble she headed for the front of the store.

'Elsie's on the warpath,' said a grinning shop assistant, grabbing the sleeve of a workmate and pointing at my mother's resolute back. The prospect of relief from boredom was irresistible so I followed.

Mum's straightforward brutality on matters of work ethic was legendary.

At home she announced her promotion to MANAGER with 'Let's see how they cope with petticoat government'.

I peeped over the GENERAL CLEANING aisle, pleased Mum had lowered the height of the aisles to survey the activities of 'thieving college students'.

A plump, stylish woman had entered the store and was removing her gloves. She held a nondescript garment wrapped loosely with tissue paper.

With head held high she scanned the store, and waited.

Mum quickly summed up the situation. 'You can't bring that back.' Mum's voice carried over the morning crowd of customers. 'You'll have to pay for it.'

The woman stalled. A red flush rose from her neck and spread. She turned to face my mother, hands fisted.

Mrs Ellmore had a reputation too, she was no shrinking violet. The room fell silent with only the chink of the cash register.

'I had this on *appro*[1],' Mrs Ellmore said, 'approved by *you*. I'm returning it.'

'Appro is four days, not "as long as you please"—you've had it for over a month. Most people can ascertain if a garment fits in five minutes, not five weeks.'

The woman stiffened. 'You do know who I am!'

This rhetorical question confused Mum who lived in a black and white world.

'Don't be ridiculous, of course I do.' Mum took the parcel, turned on her heel and walked away.

Mrs Ellmore paused, then smiled and glanced at the onlookers, who developed a sudden interest in the contents of their trolleys.

---

[1] "Appro" stands for Approval, a system where customers could take items of clothing home to try on. Garments were taken on trust – there was no payment at the time, until today's system.

The love virus

I was fourteen, he was fifteen. We were both artistic, free spirited, with hair as black as midnight. We had shared a few classes and done assignments together with quiet companionship. Then things changed. He cast long brooding looks my way, unsettling me. He didn't tease like other teenage boys—making him appear more mature. He didn't lack confidence, but he made no move to approach me—not even with the friendly mateship many of the boys offered because I played sport with them, or helped with their homework. I was confused. Why was he watching me in this new way but not talking to me?

His eyes were half mocking, half daring. My feelings and emotions were on a roller-coaster. I hadn't felt this way about a boy before. Why should I care if he ignored me? I didn't know what to do, but knew I would never go to him, also knowing one day he would find me. His intense gaze told me that.

Whenever I was near him, it took all my effort to hold a normal conversation with anyone. I walked away forgetting every word, but remembering his eyes. When I was near him, every word I said sounded wrong, and it suddenly seemed so important to get it right.

My spine tingled when I crossed the room where he was sitting casual and relaxed, watching every move I made and listening to every word. I knew he was aware of me as soon as I entered a room. I was terrified everyone would read my face and mind. I was so uncomfortable, my stomach churned. I longed for his presence, a look, a glance, but I avoided him and his knowing eyes. While he was watching a rehearsal for a school play, a romantic comedy I was in, he looked me clearly in the eyes. With a jolt I realised I loved him. Loved him and hated him, while hating myself for the feelings I could no longer control. How dare he invade my mind—my peace? I was lost. I was found.

One day while swimming in a group, I was winded and sinking under the water; struggling, terrified. He came to me then. Cradling me in his arms, he would not let me go, even long after I had caught my breath and the panic had ceased.

We were inseparable for three days, talking, sharing,

with the intensity of our unspoken feelings growing. I experienced a new kind of happiness near him, but there was a vulnerability awakened that frightened me. At times he also seemed afraid of the intensity of our connection, the fragility of our youth.

I walked home from school on air, not wanting to take the school bus and join the other jostling mortals, who knew nothing of my paradise. I lay on my bed staring at the ceiling, willing my mind to remember his face, but I could not bring it clearly to mind.

Then nothing. He went back to brooding stares and I descended to despair. I walked home, apart from the others, not wanting them to know my hell. I lay on the bed, gazing blankly at the ceiling trying to erase his face, but I could not make it recede.

Mr Sox dies and I want to grow up

Much is made of the carefree life of the Fifties and Sixties as the time of security of neighbourhoods, where everyone knew each other, a time of innocence and social safety with freedom to roam. But there was a downside.

From the echelons of the rich to the parsimony of the poor there was a dearth, a lack of explanation, a void in teaching children about life. It seemed generation after generation had learned by experience and that was how the world worked. It didn't work for our generation and many times I have wondered if it ever really had. The idea seemed to be that 'life' would bring the lessons you needed; neatly wrapped, delivered to your doorstep at just the time you needed them. No-one needed to answer questions, explain life, emotions or relationships. For me, and I suspect for many others, it was an unbearable silence that confused and complicated life. What you're not told, you guess. Some people brushed things aside, some experimented and others pursued the knowledge of themselves with exuberance via drugs, sex and Rock'n'Roll. All those things were happening at my school in muted secrets, except the only drugs referred to seem to be giggled whisperings about 'the pill' in the girls' toilets. Those who felt this silence talked of finding themselves.

The general consensus of parents was that whatever it was teens were looking for, it couldn't be good, and they'd better put a lid on the nonsense even tighter. They conferred with each other and prepared themselves for questions. They needn't have bothered. After a lifetime of sidestepping us, we weren't going to turn to them in our teens. Some of our teachers nobly tried to fill the gap, never knowing in that very class the boys were passing the latest girly magazines down the back row.

I buried myself in enough study and questioning life to 'find' a few thousand other people as well as myself. But all I found was confusion. Middle high school was supposed to be a time when the doors of enlightenment opened wide— giving life options and preparing teenagers for university and the real world. This expansion of knowledge, however, did not include how to *be* in the world, how to relate to others and how to handle emotions. The little that was said to us about emotions gave the distinct impression they were unnecessary, untrustworthy and generally to be avoided. Emotions were flaws. If they reared their ugly heads they were to be subjugated with all possible force. Bringing them up in public was akin to bringing up wind, and about as attractive. If you must have them—keep them to yourself. After all, that's what the Queen does, along with all civilised people.

I seemed to be particularly unfortunate. I was afflicted with more emotions than any self-respecting person would lay claim to. I made matters worse by seeking answers with all the zeal and persistence of Oliver Twist's quest for more porridge. I learned there was only one thing worse than the pursuit of answers, and that was to ask 'What's wrong with wanting to know stuff?'

Babies cried a lot. Children cried occasionally. Adults never cried. It was apparently something you grew out of, like the desire to suck your thumb, or take your doll everywhere.

When I was a little girl, I found my father crying piteously behind our dunny when his pet rabbit died. Ashamed of his tears he turned away from me, pushing back my words of comfort with a dismissive wave of his arm. He wanted me to leave him alone. When he came back inside we never spoke of it; this nameless thing. My world spun on its axis. Everything I thought I knew about emotions was ripped away.

A few years later, when Mum's favourite sister died she howled like a cow in labour. I wasn't allowed near her until the outpouring of her agony was past. I wanted to make her better. I stood by her door and sang her favourite song that always made her happy.

'Leave your mother alone, Linda. You're upsetting her.' Dad gently led me away from her doorway.

When she arose, dry-eyed and calm and returned to the housework we never spoke of it; this nameless thing. The world went from turning on its axis to spinning out of control. How could such strong feelings disappear so quickly?

When I was fourteen I called my beloved cat, Mr. Sox, to

come home from across the road. He was hit by a car. I screamed blue murder as he lay there lifeless and bloodied. I ran to the place Dad had gone to cry. The dunny was long gone. I threw myself into the gully nearby.

Although never previously having shown affection for me, Snoopy, my brother's dog, licked me and leant on me, resting his head gently on my sobbing shoulder. It took a "dumb animal" to know what to do with that nameless thing called grief. I held him with vice-like fingers, howling in agony, wondering when the magic of growing up happened and emotions left you alone.

Then dad came and held me firmly, offering me the comfort he couldn't accept for himself.

Country 'Snobs'

Our school was a country school. Those of us who hadn't travelled far, and that was most of us, didn't know any other way of life. All schools must be like ours.

Occasionally we had students who had come from The Mission Field. We gathered around these new people with glee, bombarding them with questions about foreign places. We found them universally reluctant to share their past lives with us. After we'd nagged them, we received a few unintelligible, mumbled phrases. Any further pestering ended in the Mission children telling us they wanted to forget all about wherever they'd been. We were a bunch of 'sticky beaks' and should leave them alone. We decided The Mission Field must have been akin to Prison of War camps—such was their angst at our questions.

Later of course, much later, we realised they just wanted to fit in and be like us. Our constant calling attention to their previous lives only made them feel as if they would never fit in. We locals had known each other all our lives and had no concept of 'fitting in' other than a strong desire not to be picked last for rounders, not to cry in front of the others and woe upon woes—never wet our pants. Some things could be lived down, but not that. If anyone suffered that dreadful fate, they had our undying sympathy, but in social terms—they might as well emigrate.

I knew nothing of aborigines, their customs or heritage. It was a long time before I stumbled on that most basic fact that 'they were here first'. Because Peter claimed all television viewing rights due to seniority I'd watched many Westerns so I had an idea about American Indians, and immediately transposed their history to our indigenous people. I was enchanted by the lives of the 'redskins' and their culture and once spent an entire hot, slow Sunday begging Mum to change my name to Pocahontas because "Linda" was boring.

With that background it was only natural that I desired to embrace my aboriginal compatriots. Or I would have, but I didn't lay eyes on a single one until I was 14 and in high school. Sadly, my new prospective aboriginal friend didn't like the look of me. There was no embracing to be had with the only aborigine of my acquaintance. I must have seemed like an over-exuberant puppy and scared the poor kid.

Anything we saw on television was American and gave us very little idea of our own country beyond our small town experience. We thought ourselves privileged indeed to have Dora Creek. It didn't occur to us to hold the dirty old Dora in disdain. After all, she was all we had—only movie stars had swimming pools. If we came out of the water looking like woolly mammoths because the marmite detritus stuck to the finest of our body hair, we didn't complain.

Our school swimming "experiences" also took place in

the muddy Dora, not far from the swing bridge. I use the word experiences, because no-one actually taught us to swim. This was a source of great anxiety for me. On our family holidays I'd been able to fake the whole swimming process, just managing an awkward dog-paddle. However, here at the creek where the teachers would assess our swimming skills, it was a whole new ball game. One where humiliation was my only possible destination. I prayed for a sudden onset of smallpox.

Our teacher, Mr Solomon, lined us up on one side of the creek and was going to watch us swim across. Except that in my case he was going to watch me drown. The first half a dozen to arrive at the other side would be chosen to compete in The Swimming Carnival. 'We're going to compete with Strathfield High School this year.'

'Oh great! City snobs,' I moaned.

'Keep that up Brooks, and you'll be sent back to school,' he threatened. Oh the joy—escape was possible. I only had to up the ante, give a bit more attitude and I'd be sent back to school. No-one would ever know my dark secret.

'Well, they are snobs, Mr Solomon. When they came here for our last Sports Day all they did was look down their noses at us. Isn't that the definition of 'snob' Mr Solomon? Isn't it?' I silently prayed for release, the long walk back to school, a thousand years detention—anything but the revelation I'd spent years in water without making significant progress through it, unable to acquit myself at 'freestyle', faked or not, which was a crucial requirement.

'Be quiet and line up in the water with the others,

Brooks.'

'But sir! Don't I get sent back to school?'

'No.'

'But you said!'

'Line up!'

My doom was sealed. The water was too deep to fake a crossing. I looked for a log. Perhaps I could hide behind it and sneak away. The other kids were squealing with excitement, thrilled at the thought of being chosen. I felt sick to my stomach. I was going to sink like a stone. Solomon blew the whistle. The muddy waters of the creek foamed with the thrashing arms of dozens of kids. There were screams of delight as Solomon officially announced the winners who had earned the marvellous honour of representing the school. Cheers filled the air. 'Alright you lot! Now swim back here and collect your gear.'

I didn't move. I scarcely dared breathe. I couldn't believe Solomon hadn't noticed that I was on the wrong side of the creek, having never left. The kids were so excited, noisily splashing their way back, that for the first time in my school days, I escaped detection. After arriving at the original side the kids began to scramble out and grab their clothes and towels. Solomon looked down at me with a quizzical expression. 'Brooks, get a move on! Get out of the water! We haven't got all day!'

'Yes sir!' I crowed, dizzy with relief.

The day of The Carnival came. We pretended not to see the shiny city bus. Our mouths were open with shock when the children stepped down from the bus adorned with hats and gloves. We looked down at our scruffy shoes, laces askew. They lined up in perfect straight lines. We remembered being called 'higgledy-piggledy brown's cows' and shuddered. A few of the pristine Strathfield girls whispered and giggled quietly.

'Silence, please!' said an elegant teacher as she inspected the lines of children. Our eyes popped. Their 'noise' would have been considered good behaviour to our teachers. We had an inkling why we were often called a 'rowdy lot'. One teacher had even declared he'd met heathens with better manners.

Our city counterparts eyed us as one would a group of feral animals. This would not do at all! We girls huddled together. We had to defend ourselves against these distant, superior invaders. We devised cunning replies and prepared cutting barbs. We needn't have bothered. None of them deigned to speak to us.

Don't kiss me, I like it!

Boys started using tough guy tactics to get a girl's attention long before movies made irresistible heroes out of angry, macho men. On my first day at school I casually walked past the monkey-bars. They were useless junk in my opinion. Having tried them once I had no inclination to go there again. Some rude boy, who was sitting at the top of them decided to introduce himself to me in the time-honoured manner of 'the caveman'.

'You can't come up here! You're a girl! Girls aren't allowed up here,' he called down to me.

'Says who?'

'Says me! That's who!'

'Ha!' I climbed to the top of the monkey-bars, knocked him to the ground then never went near the bloody things again. It was the principle.

When I arrived in high school, I was still shockingly naïve of the workings of the male/female attraction dynamic. By Year 8 the girls had geared up to a serious level of worshipping the opposite sex. Typically this obsession began with plastering bedroom walls with posters of various male television stars or singing idols. Even though I was prepared to make some effort to gain social acceptance, the idea of adoring a complete stranger made no sense to me at all. Then the girls discovered the boys right under their noses and began serious attempts to get their attention. After all, they were more attainable—at least in theory.

Even though I wasn't immune to the teenage male of the species, the method of getting together with the object of your desire involved many dubious processes, including note passing. This required a higher level of trust than I was able to achieve. If the teacher didn't intercept the note, some sneaky kid grabbed it before it reached its destination. Some poor girl's humiliation was complete, followed by inevitable crying in the toilets.

Another method was using friends to act as intermediaries. This appeared even more disastrous due to the tendency of the messenger to deliver the message to the wrong boy, or even worse, announcing the message to the class accompanied by much snickering, making the girl the object of public ridicule. This led to more crying in the toilets. This crying was often a group activity necessitating several or more sympathizers to comfort the hapless victim. Most of the girls seemed to find this outpouring of grief cathartic, but I was horrified.

I found many of the girls couldn't be trusted with your deepest secrets, especially if they had aspirations in the same direction. When I was approached by anyone begging me to tell them which boy I liked, promise I won't tell, I told them to buzz off. This amused the boys immensely and they let me play sport with them, even though my usefulness was limited. This arrangement annoyed the girls and they wouldn't let me near them.

I remember one torrid school day that must have followed a full moon. There had been so many protestations of undying love, followed by rejection, that I was the only girl sitting in the geography class after lunch break.

'Where's Amanda? Do you know where she is, Brooks?' Mr Grosse asked. I squirmed under the interrogation, worried about my tendency to put my foot in my mouth.

'In the toilet crying, Sir,' I responded. The boys looked confused.

'Where's Felicity?'

'In the toilet, crying too.'

'Did someone die, Brooks?'

'No, sir.'

'Well, where are the rest of the girls?'

'In the toilets too, sir.'

'Are they all crying, Brooks?'

'No sir. A couple of 'em are. They don't like crying

alone.'

Mr Grosse looked confused. I was confused. I only ever cried in the presence of my cat. Crying didn't occur very often at our house, and it was definitely never a group activity.

'What the heck are they crying about?' he persisted.

I mumbled and wriggled in my chair. The nagging feeling I might have already said too much assailed me. I shrugged my shoulders in what I hoped was a non-committal manner.

'Why aren't you crying, Brooks?'

'I'm not crying over some stupid boy, sir!'

The boys laughed. I blushed. Now I knew I'd said too much.

'Keep it up, Brooks,' said Mr Grosse succinctly, as if I'd just passed a difficult Maths exam. After class that morning he gave me a simple life lesson I never forgot.

'You've got potential, Brooks. We teachers see girls come to high school and they do well for the first year. Then they discover boys.'

'What do you mean 'discover' them?'

'Let me put it like this, they get "boy mad". They forget about their schoolwork and all their hard work goes down the drain. It's very discouraging for teachers.'

'Oh, you won't have to worry about me, Mr Grosse. That doesn't run in our family.'

'Good for you. I think you'll make it.'

I walked away quite chuffed. I'd been given a really useful clue about life and not just equations and topography. I didn't think it was worth bothering anyway, because so many school romances ended in tears before they began.

Later in Year 9 when I developed a crush on a boy in the class above, I discovered that when it came to communicating with the opposite sex, I was no better than anyone else. Year 9 and 10 classes went on a combined Science excursion to the nearby lakeside scrounging around for plant life, also known as the collection of flora specimens. I was thrilled when Elliot, the object of my teenage desire, asked to partner me in the project.

Somehow we became separated from the main group, and he took the opportunity to grab me and plant a smacking kiss on the back of my neck. I was furious. Not because he'd kissed me, but because it was my first kiss and it was all over in a split second. This wasn't how it was supposed to happen. I'd seen the midday movies. Kisses were supposed to be conducted in a completely different manner.

I was monumentally disappointed. Where were the tender looks? Lips meeting willing lips. I didn't even have the chance to participate. Elliot merely stood back, arms folded, with a sickening smirk of triumph on his face. I wanted to whack him. The more I glared the more he grinned, so I stalked off, heartedly disillusioned. He'd been a caveman and I'd wanted to slap him.

Romance grows up and so do I

When I reached my mid-teens I suddenly became aware that my brother, Peter, had a few mates with movie-star good looks. Finally, having a big brother was going to work for me. I already had entry to the world of the shed.

I would sit on the bench next to the circular saw or vice. My heart would race a little faster as his mates gathered around the car engines, yahooing and discussing the stuff of men and machines.

Surely they would notice me sooner or later, I thought, as I sat there waiting to receive some kind of romantic attention. It would have to happen someday. I didn't bother to preen or fuss—I didn't want to be too obvious.

One day I decided to up the ante. I took a bit more time with my hair, even practicing some newly-acquired makeup techniques.

I was hopeful they'd notice the change. I held my breath, smiling warmly.

The guys sauntered in, chatted a while, then prepared to leave. Peter walked past me, ruffling my hair.

'See ya later, Sis.'

My heart thumped in as the other guys walked past.

'See ya later, Sis,' they said grinning, also ruffling my

hair. Oh the rejection. I cried the makeup off my stricken face.

'Geez, sis! What happened to you? Looks like you went a few rounds with Mohammed Ali,' said Peter later.

'Oh shut up!' I said.

A new family arrived in town with four sons.

'Have you seen the new boys?' wafted Jennifer dreamily. 'They're divine. So many of them, and all gorgeous.' She sighed, wriggling sublimely further back on the school bench. 'I think one is going to be in Year 10 with us. Did you see them at church?'

'Yes, I have. They *are* gorgeous and divine, but they're probably all up themselves,' I replied.

'You're a hopeless case Linda, how do you expect to get a boyfriend?'

'What's with 'expect'? There's no use 'expecting' boyfriends. There *is no* Prince Charming and no Cinderella.'

'Don't you ever want to fall in love?'

'Sure. But when I do, I want it to be in love with someone who isn't more in love with himself than me.'

'You don't even know them.'

'Maybe not, but what I do know is that I'm going to study, have a career and Mr. Blooming Right had better understand.'

'You mean you want to be a corporate brainchild?'

'No! I just don't ever want to be completely dependent on a man.'

'But that's what love is all about!' Jennifer gave me a

pitying glance. 'You don't make sense.'

'Hardly ever try to,' I responded.

Bored with the conversation and the adoration of boys I turned back to my Science book. Jennifer went to find more amenable females to join her worship. She didn't have to look far.

The two oldest sons were going to College and two were coming to high school. You couldn't help but know these things because it was all the girls talked about. I went to the library for peace and studied Maths with some of the boys I'd played cricket with in Primary School. They treated me as an equal and were good mates.

The new boys arrived and one was in Year 10. Handsome and charming, Andrew was an instant hit—you could almost tell where he was by the female sighs. He was in the French class with me. We were soon knee-deep in conversation about the universe and sharing study time.

In year 11 his older brother Gary arrived at high school. The sighing began again. He had been at college the year before, but had decided to repeat Year 11 'to get better grades'.

'So he's dumb,' I said, to the consternation of the other girls.

There were cries of aiming higher and I soon tired of the whole thing, retreating to somewhere quiet. Along with some other teens I was introduced to him at church the next week. He looked straight through me and didn't say a word. He was different from Andrew with his open face and clear-eyed view of life. Gary had a dark shadow, an 'edgy' indifference.

'Arrogant prat,' I said to Jennifer who was fluttering her eyes at all of them and no one in particular.

'He's probably just shy,' said Jennifer, ever willing to see the best in everyone.

'*Shy my bum!* He's been eyeing off every pair of legs and boobs since he got here.'

'Linda!'

Jennifer was relieved when I went to find Mum and Dad, but not as relieved as I was.

While the younger brother Andrew had accepted overtures from the girls graciously, not appearing to favour anyone above the others; Gary was a different story. Being older he had a car and plenty of attitude to go with it. He was never without a girlfriend, each new girl adoring him with a simpering submissiveness that was nauseating.

I couldn't stand him. He had a girlfriend when he arrived, one of the secretaries from a local business, but that didn't stop him from playing up to nearly every female he met. He was democratic with his lavish charm at school and I cut his legs off every time he spoke to me after finding subtlety ineffective.

Things came to a head when one of my closest friends was having a birthday party at a local diner. There was a clearing in the bushland, where a bonfire was organised after the meal.

Gary came with Andrew and a group of friends. Games were organised for the after-dinner fireside fun. I was standing near a group of trees after the meal, when Gary and his group gathered near his car.

'Let's get the hell out of here now the meal's over,' he said, heading to his car. Andrew headed for the bonfire.

'We can't leave now! It would be rude to eat and run.'

Gary glared at him and continued towards the car.

'At least let me go to say happy birthday and thanks,' protested Andrew.

'Don't be a drip. We're going.'

Just as they neared the car I stepped out from behind a tree. Gary looked at me with my arms crossed.

'So, pretty Linda. How're you doing?'

'I'm fine, thanks,' I murmured softly. 'A whole lot better than a rude arrogant pig like you.'

He stopped in his tracks, eyes narrowing.

He was well over six foot and looked down at me. I held his gaze with indignant fiery eyes. After sucking in a shocked breath, he was ready to try again.

'That's what girls say when they're interested in a guy,' he murmured, lowering his head towards me.

'It's *also* what girls say when they think a guy is a rude arrogant pig. I wouldn't expect you to know the difference—how many years will you be 'getting better grades'? If you don't watch out, you'll still be in school with your children.'

He yelled at his friends, stormed to the car and took off in a spray of gravel. Furious, I went to find the birthday girl and tell her they'd gone, leaving out the conversation. That'd fix him, I thought, he'll leave me alone now. But I was wrong; the next day at school he showed an even more determined attitude.

'Sexy shoes, Linda.' He passed me as I sat reading a book.

'Aren't they though...' I responded breathlessly. '...they're called Shin-kickers. Fancy a demonstration?'

He kept grinning while I went back to my reading, fuming.

Gary kept up the running gambit and was actually without a girlfriend for a time. I gave no sharp words unless he made a provocative remark, but when he did I was ready for him.

'Why do you bite my head off, Linda?' he asked once.

We'd been assigned to do a Science project together.

'I don't like sleazy remarks.'

A red flush crept over his shocked face.

'But I...none of the other girls...' he stopped in confusion.

'But I'm not...' I began sharply.

'Like any of the others,' he finished.

'Congratulations Gary! You might actually pass an exam one distant day.'

'I'd rather pass...'

'Don't ruin it.'

It was a truce of sorts. After that he certainly treated me differently, asking for help with class work and pulling out a chair for me to pass. One day he turned to Jennifer who was sitting in a double desk with me.

'Jennifer,' he began subtly, 'Can I swap seats with you?'

'Oh sure, Gary,' she demurred. I looked up quickly.

'*Oh really!*' I spat out. 'That would mean you would be

sitting with me, Gary. As if! If you think I'm going to be one of those stupid girls, who sit with you, then cries buckets over you, you can think again. I'm not even sure I could cry at your funeral without an onion. If you swap with Jennifer, I won't be sitting here when you get here!'

I looked at Jennifer in disgust over her collusion.

'You'd put your head in the oven over a stupid boy,' I growled. I spun back on Gary.

'If manipulation is the only way you know to get girls, you'd better stick to dummies because it's disrespectful. If you want something you need to man up.'

Nobody changed seats. Gary apologised later with a gentleness that showed a crack of sincerity.

I accepted the apology, but with little grace so he wouldn't ask again, but he was challenged by my indifference. I had the measure of him and he began to show a new kind of respect.

He began a whole new campaign of gentleness. The barriers I had built around my heart began to crumble and I saw pain beyond the cocky attitude, sensitivity behind the rebellion.

I was young, idealistic and vulnerable. I was used to being responsible at home, comforting Mum and Dad when my brother's hooligan antics had them at their wit's end. They were confused and pained when his rebellion kicked into full flight.

Whenever I was tiny and I asked Mum if she loved me she said, 'Don't ask silly questions, Linda. Everything I do is because I love you and Peter and Dad. A mother feels every pain her children feel. You'll know when you're a mother.' This seemed lacking; I longed to hear the words more often, especially when under her chastening rod.

She was wrong about one thing. I didn't have to wait to become a mother to understand about the constricting pain of mother love, for I was her companion in the darkest valley of her life, when my brother came face to face with the consequences of his teenage recklessness.

Mum wept openly and unrestrained. I held her in my arms. Between wrenching sobs she cried, 'Why don't they tear the clothes from my back and lash the whip on me? It would be easier to bear. What sort of mother am I?' For a time she seemed to be drowning. All Dad and I could do to ease her heartache was to take her place in the world, for she no longer had any use for it.

Silently, Dad passed the pegs while I hung the clothes. Quietly huddled together we did the shopping and the household chores while Mum lay in despair. We went to church, where Dad kept a dignified vigil at the sound system.

At school I bore the withdrawal of past friends; taunted daily by one of the girls. There was sympathy in the eyes of the others, but none stood boldly to stop the cruel words. Their silence squeezed my heart more than her words did. My passion for the underdog was fired in that crucible. My lips would not be the ones to fall silent.

After the storm passed Mum pretended everything was fine, as if nothing had ever happened. Maybe if she acted the part well enough it would become real. I didn't understand this pretence in my raw heart. Nothing would be 'fine' for a long time. I was confused about so many things, but I knew I was no longer child.

I understood all her earlier words then; of mother's pain, of protecting care. I knew the depth of her love, her awkward yearning heart. She was a hard-working country mother, with stoic heart, who demonstrated love by deed and action. Seeing this vulnerable side of both my parents drew me closer to them. Their quiet defeat and mute agony affected me deeply. I vowed there would be no heart scald for them with my name on it. I vowed never to betray their trust in me.

Gary and I grew closer as he let his barriers down. His desire to rebel seemed to mellow with my friendship.

Changes in him became more noticeable. He wore his curly hair in an afro, which in the Seventies grieved his parents and the teachers. We were swimming at school and I laughed when he came out of the water shaking his hair.

'What are you laughing at?' he asked, accustomed to adulation for his blonde locks and bronzed frame.

'You look like a poodle—a skinny, knock-kneed poodle.'

'Cut my hair for me!'

'Okay.' So I did. When he arrived home his parents were astonished, because all their pleading had fallen on deaf ears. The rebel had been tamed. They were eager to meet me.

He told me he loved me, saying the words I wanted to hear.

'I love you, not for who you are, but for what you are

making of me.'

My heart swelled. To a born rescuer, those words were the lyric of being needed. It seemed the ultimate accolade. I was making him want to be a better man.

I guess you're wondering what happened. I found that as a relationship choice, rescuing someone was the equivalent of walking into a war zone with no weapons, armour or strategy. When it was over, I needed more rescuing than he ever had.

Then I saw what I had dreaded most—heartache in my parents' eyes that bore my name. But there were no words of reproach or regret to me, just compassion and protective love. My gentle father was ready to go to battle for me and my belligerent little mother said, 'Not if I get there first, Max.'

Sometimes I think of the words Gary said that sealed my love, 'I love you, not for who you are, but for what you are making of me'. How would I respond to those same words today?

Run like hell.

'We're breaking out!'

'I'm going to sneak you out of the house at midnight,' he whispered.

I groaned.

This casual conversation had been rambling around for hours. My brother, Peter, and I used to sit up late and chat on the rare occasions when he and his 'devil-may-care' mates didn't have anything planned for Saturday night. Sometimes we'd chat after he'd driven to town with them or they'd just lairised the neighbourhood.

On these occasions, I thought it was good to get a bit of

an inside look into the way the male brain worked. Surely, there was something brothers were remotely useful for. His stories usually made my hair stand on end. His driving alone would scare ten years growth off anybody. I enjoyed having these chats, naively believing, quite falsely I might add, that I'd learn something about men.

However, I learned a fair bit about boys who showed little sign of ever actually attaining manhood. Already established as 'hoods', I thought it was dubious any of them would ever earn any level of 'man-hood'. But what the hell, I was bored, so I went along with some of his tamer adventures, like hanging off the back of one or other of his 'bush-basher' cars or a rebuilt motor bike.

The suggestion of sneaking me out of the house was part of his plan to make me live a little, It was my strong opinion that any of his larks would make me die a little. There were only three and a half years between us, but there might as well have been three generations the other way around, because I often thought he had the common sense of a gnat. He, on the other hand, believed I was in grave danger of becoming 'boring' and had justifiably earned the title of 'goody two shoes'. A title I was never been offended by, no matter the source.

Peter knew his chances of me going to some of the places he frequented to be minimal. I strongly doubted my presence would have been welcome in any case. His carefully hatched idea, (all of three nanoseconds in the planning) was to show me the excitement of leaving the comfort of your own residence in the dead of night undetected.

This was a great load of nonsense to me, as Dad was notorious for 'sleeping like a log' and Mum was already well on the road to being 'hard of hearing'.

'I don't know why you don't just walk out the back door when you slope off with your mates in the middle of the night. No-one would hear you anyway. Seems pretty stupid to climb out a window, if you ask me.'

Peter merely looked at me as if I was a 'spaz', a term much bandied around by him and his mates. I won't elucidate any of the others, because I very often missed their precise meaning, but the guffawing that accompanied their vocabulary left little to the imagination. I pretended these things went over my head, which wasn't hard. After all, little sisters were considered 'persona non gratis' much of the time.

The escape would occur at midnight. Apparently it would broaden my mind to take a risk in life. I forbore telling him it was harder to climb the back fence than go down a ladder from my own bedroom window, so on a scale of danger this 'escape' scored poorly indeed.

'Daft, that's what you are,' I declared.

Now this is where the farce kicks in. Peter was assisting me to climb out of my window so that I could climb into his window to watch television all night. So basically, the destination of the whole adventure was another room in the house. We were 'breaking out' to break back in where we came from.

I agreed with this scheme partly because I couldn't quite

believe this was the best he could do to enhance the sad, boring life of a sister with the unfathomable defect of liking homework.

My parents ruled the television with iron fisted tyranny; in theory. The truth was that with their long working hours we watched what we liked. Well, to be entirely honest, we watched exactly what Peter liked. This meant I had to sit through such stunning masterpieces as The Lone Ranger (who wasn't really 'lone'), Wyatt Earp, The Adams Family and any other load of rubbish Peter found appealing. I preferred watching musicals with Dad, but to Peter this was 'lame'. He thought he was doing me a great service by trying to cultivate my viewing tastes. Anyway, TV was the 'raison d'être' for our adventure.

Watching television all night as the pinnacle of rebellion, failed on every level to appeal to me. It was hard enough to sit through afternoon telly viewing with Peter, when I would rather have been sewing, doing my homework or sticking pins in my eyes. But life is full of compromise and for the sole purpose of pleasing my brother I went along with the 'breaking out' nonsense. After all, I was leaving home soon and would miss the big lout. Of course, I would never have told him how much I cherished our late night talks. Sisters had a tendency to be far too 'sappy' for brothers on the verge of manhood.

The escapade nearly fell apart before it began. We only had one TV in the lounge room, so it had to be shifted to Peter's room, because the lounge room was right next to Mum and Dad's bedroom. Now there was already an underground running war over the telly. In order to maintain control Dad removed the valves whenever he wasn't home to avoid any inappropriate viewing. The excellence of this scheme came undone because Peter had his own set of valves, which he inserted and removed at his leisure, giving him the freedom to watch whatever he liked. I don't know if Dad ever caught on to this malarkey.

On this night, Peter quite cleverly relocated the telly to his room at about 10 pm. It was conspicuous by its absence, which would have been fine except that Dad had not retired to bed as we thought, but was working late in the shed. When I heard him come inside, my pudding heart thundered in my chest. Help! Dad would notice the telly missing. There'd be trouble. I trembled in my bed. Already exhausted by the late hour, not to mention reluctant, I decided a life of deception did not appeal. I don't know why I was worried about 'trouble'. I'd never heard Dad raise his voice. Dad only had to look disappointed to soften my heart—an affliction obviously not shared by my heathen brother.

Peter, who was lurking in his room, decided to head Dad off at the pass. He casually sauntered into the lounge room where Dad had unfortunately decided to have a late night read before heading to bed. Peter sat down opposite Dad and started some meaningless conversation with him, so Dad wouldn't notice the empty corner with wires leading to Peter's room. Now, Dad was not a stupid man in anyone's books, but he didn't notice the missing telly—perhaps because this was the first time in living history that Peter, son and heir, had shown interest in having a normal everyday conversation with his long-suffering parent. Dad was clearly in shock.

I was dozing fretfully when Peter tapped on my bedroom window, demolishing all hope he'd forget the nonsense. The only thing I wanted to see was the inside of my eyelids, but the law of seniority prevailed. I climbed out of my window, down the ladder, then into Peter's window, making more noise in the process than if the local fire brigade had arrived. Incredibly, both Mum and Dad slept through the whole nerve-wracking episode. After all, they both worked long hard hours.

What followed was the most boring night of my life and possibly the longest. Late night television was obviously invented for the terminally bored, stupid, and possibly criminally insane. One of the movies featured a graphic account of the End of The World, which at that moment was looking better than the prospect of another minute of television. Just before dawn Peter began to snore like a chainsaw, so I escaped to my room—walking quietly through the house. Let Clever Clogs Peter work out the problem of the ladder, the telly, the valves, wires and whatever else needed replacing.

'See Sis! Wasn't that fun!' he declared cheerfully the next morning over Cornflakes. I gave him a filthy look.

'You're retarded,' I said, with a dearth of patience common to the bitterly sleep deprived.

The patience of the Saints

Slam!

'What did you go and do that for, Dad?' I complained.

His large, booted foot had planted itself on top of mine on the brake while we were out on a driving lesson. I'd had my L's for a month, but Dad still had an alarming habit of grabbing the wheel or slamming his foot on the brakes from the passenger side of the car.

'Get out,' he said, rather less calmly than usual.

'Oh great, here we go again! Really Dad, I don't know why you panic when I'm behind the wheel.'

'Because you *don't* panic, that's why!'

'But Dad, why don't you have confidence in me? I've been driving a go-cart for years?' A groan was Dad's only reply. We were at the main intersection into Morisset and the humiliating swap that was becoming part of the routine for my driving lessons.

We drove home in silence. By the time we reached the garage his rattled nerves had abated and I went into the kitchen to whine to Mum. Here, I had a sympathetic audience at least.

'Oh dear,' she said, rolling her eyes, 'I remember *that* when your father taught me. I'd be sailing along nicely out comes your father's arm from nowhere and pulls the car to the side of the road. 'I'll take over now Else' he'd say. Took all my confidence I can tell you.'

'Did he squash your foot leaning over to slam on the brakes?'

'Don't remind me.' she groaned again. We looked out of the kitchen window to where Dad had retreated to the shed.

The next Sunday, we started out with me promising to be cautious and slow, while Dad quietly resolved not to lose his patience—not that he said it, I could see it in his eyes. I knew the length of his patience depended on my ability to drive in the same methodical slow manner he did, but as much as I vowed to get it right, before we'd gone more than a few miles, trouble started. I swung into the main street of Morisset confidently at the T section. Bam! Dad was at it again.

'You didn't have time to get around that corner,' he

remonstrated.

'What do you mean I didn't have time? We're here aren't we? We're not dead! There was no accident—all things that would have happened if I didn't have time.' My logic failed to impress my father who declared me 'an argumentative little minx', before swapping seats to return home.

'I'm never going to learn to drive,' I muttered mutinously.

'I'm never going to see old age,' he riposted, the hint of a sparkle in his eyes.

My boyfriend said looking at me in the driver's seat gave him the heebie-jeebies and refused to even contemplate the task of teaching me. This made no sense to me, because when he was driving he had a terrifying habit of making me grab the wheel while he scratched his foot. Usually when we were tearing down the highway at a million miles an hour.

Dad gave up. I waited until I earned my own money and hired a professional driving instructor. He was a volatile Pakistani who found me every bit as annoying as Dad and my boyfriend.

'You silly Australia girl! Why don't you wait for other cars?' he screeched, nerves jangling, on our first lesson.

'They were standing still! Why wait for cars that aren't moving?' I argued.

My instructor was incensed. With a shy wife he was not accustomed to females who answered back—he found my brashness particularly unappealing. With shaking hands, he lit a cigarette. I felt a pang of guilt; I'd taken pity on lesser men.

'Why does not your boyfriend teach you?' he asked.

I chose not to dignify this question with a response on the grounds that it might incriminate me.

I wound the window down. The freezing air dispersed his cigarette smoke, but this further annoyed him. 'What's wrong with you, girl? Why be winding down the window in the middle of winter?' he yelled.

'I can't stand smoke.'

He gave me a look that could kill. This was how we went - the nervy cranky Pakistani abusing me—and the obnoxious schoolgirl, debating every point. He lit cigarettes while I hacked false coughs, repeatedly winding the window down.

'Smoking will kill you, you know?' I said one evening when I was tired, and sick of the freezing air.

'Someone like you will kill me before smoking does!'

'You seem *very* stressed,' I responded with mock kindness.

He answered in a stream of his own language where I was sure the word maniac featured.

It was time for my driving test. My teacher was not remotely confident I had a chance in hell of getting my license, but there was one thing he was sure about—he'd had enough of me. I saw him in the mirror as I took off with the large gentle policeman who was testing me. My Pakistani instructor was waving his arms in despair. Apparently I'd make a mistake already. Only 100 yards down the road I stalled at the first set of lights. The policeman was a patient, kind soul with nerves of steel. Of course he must have been to take students through the city daily for their driving tests.

When we arrived back I received a warm handshake from the large officer and my new license. My Pakistani instructor was torn between astonishment and rage. He drove me home.

'Never in my 36 years…' he mumbled.

When we arrived home, I gave him a sweet smile and said I was going to be a nurse. I told him if he was ever a patient I would look after him with great care. His wide eyes white with terror, he tore off down the road.

'Bad tempered git,' I muttered, then was struck with remorse because my own gentle father had given up on driving lessons.

Mum's Get Rich Schemes

'You could help me, Linda,' Mum said, waving a piece of paper. 'There's a fete at the community centre. They have all sorts of stalls. We could do with the extra money. You're good at all kinds of things.'

'But you never sell everything you make. That's hardly profitable.'

Mum handed me the paper. 'It would be lovely to do something together,' she said. 'You're always making something anyway. Why not pool our resources. We might make a bit of money, you never know.'

I rolled my eyes. 'Sounds like a *get rich slow scheme* to me.'

'Trust you to be sarcastic.'

'Oh Mum, it's a lot of work. Aren't retired people supposed to slow down?'

'Don't be silly. Slow down and you die.'

'See this,' she jabbed the page. 'We could have a stall. We could do arts and crafts.'

'Yeah, we all know that leads to untold wealth.'

Mum's eyes narrowed. 'You can't just bury your talents in the ground,' she said.

'I know what I could bury in the ground,' I said.

Thankfully, due to my mother's poor hearing she didn't

catch this remark.

'They only take five percent of your profits, that's fair.' Mum smiled triumphantly. 'You'll see.'

I pulled a face. Or maybe you'll see I thought, imagining Mum discovering the futility of hours spent over a sewing machine, knitting or crocheting. 'All right, let's do it,' I said. 'But I can't…'

'No such word as can't.'

'People to have limitations, Mum.'

'Rubbish, limitations are for lazy people. Let's start. Here's what I think…'

While I refused to spend all day at a stall selling, I overlocked facecloths so she could crochet around them. I made aprons, bibs and, back opening shirts for 'the elderly'. Mum had stalls at markets. She held stalls in the main street. But I put my foot down at that malarkey. Mum came up with an endless array of handcrafts. We shopped for materials.

'Jeez, Mum. This stuff costs more than we'd make on it.'

Mum gave me The Look.

Mum was ever inventive with her schemes. I decided that it was time to get on board completely and see the next scheme through to its inevitable failure. So when she approached me with a newspaper and pointed to an ad for newspaper and junk mail delivery I pulled out all the stops. If she was shocked at my apparent enthusiasm, she didn't say a word. She was elated.

Mum bought a notebook. She phoned the woman. We

picked up our papers, and were given a territory. We folded the papers and set off. 'Crikey,' said Mum when we arrived at a hilly area 45 minutes from home. 'Oh, well, I guess we have to prove ourselves and get a better area later.'

I said nothing. Any success I might have had in putting and end to these Get Rich Slow Schemes depended on my keeping my mouth shut and letting Mum work it out for herself.

We sat in the car and worked out how to cover the territory, poring over the street directory. I drove, did my bit of letterboxing and then met her. This was going very well.

Mum was triumphant.

After four hours we finished the territory and I was sitting quietly in the car waiting for her to arrive when I looked in the rear vision mirror.

Mum appeared over the top of the hill. My mouth dropped open. She was running down the hill, sprinting towards some invisible finish line. I had never seen my mother run. However, it was soon apparent why – a huge, loping German Shepherd was on her heels, barking and snapping.

I backed the car, reached over and opened the door. Mum leapt into the car, wheezing like there was no tomorrow.

The dog pawed at the window. Mum poked her tongue out at it. I'd never seen her do THAT either.

'That's one cranky animal. We'll avoid that house in future,' I said.

Mum blushed. 'It wasn't at a house. I ... er...'

'What the…?'

'Well,' said Mum. 'I had to *go*. You know. Brisk walking does that…'

'Oh,' I said as light dawned.

'Number 2?'

'Yes.'

'How did you wipe…'

'With my undies.'

'Oh my, that's why you're hanging on to your dress.'

'Yes,' she said.

We laughed uncontrollably. We laughed until we cried. We couldn't stop. I couldn't shake the image of my mother hiding in the bush, burying her undies and being found by a dog who gave chase. Every time we drew breath and thought we had our mirth under control, we started again.

'Let's just go home, Mum.'

'On no,' she said. 'I never leave a job unfinished.'

'You just proved that,' I said, as we fell about laughing again.

Mum insisted we take the papers back to the women. We both got out. We still couldn't stop laughing. It was a windy day and Mum fought to hold her dress 'I'm going to carry spare nickers after this,' she said.

I was of the opinion we presented a ridiculous pair and should throw the handful of papers in the bin back home, but Mum wouldn't hear of it.

We leaned on the supervisor's rendered brick fence for many minutes still unable to compose ourselves. When I declared I was leaving, Mum pulled herself up straight, grabbed her dress tightly and with head held high marched down the path.

I waited in the car. Mum came back and got out her notebook. Her calculations didn't take long – she was a Maths Whizz.

'What did we make?' I asked.

'Well, if we take out petrol … 50 cents each.'

School ends; a new horizon beckons

I turned 18 on the day of my Year 12 Geography exam. It was my last exam for the Higher School Certificate and would determine my entrance status to University, but I had already been accepted for registered nurse training in a prestigious private hospital in Sydney.

There left only one thing to do at school; 'Muck Up Day'. On our last day, we arrived with bags of flour in our school bags. This was a school-sanctioned event, but only Year 12 students were allowed to be involved in the shenanigans. It was a time-honoured practice that mucking up would begin after first class and last until we went home. We were allowed home at lunch time, as much for the peace of mind of the teachers, as for our early liberation.

There was no graduation ceremony or school Formal, as is common today, so all our energies were directed to creating mayhem on 'muck up day'. This year promised to be a beauty. The boys had come up with an elaborate secret plan. None of the Year 12 class could settle down for first period.

Only ten minutes into the lesson the loudspeaker crackled. It was an LP recording over the Public Address system and was being delivered to every room in the school—loudly. The recording was of a current popular comedian renowned for his extraordinary ability to imitate the sounds of machinery, trains, ferries and a wide variety of animals. We were delighted.

A couple of the teachers panicked and flew to the principal's office. This was defiant anarchy and had to be stopped immediately. Imagine their shock on arriving at the office to find that none of the controls were of any use.

They ran to the individual classrooms trying to turn the sound off, also without success. All of Year 12 was present and accounted for and feigning sublime ignorance.

The teachers were flummoxed. A student of the previous year, who was an electronic whiz, had rewired the whole Public Address system and was controlling it from a well-hidden spot under the school building.

Our Maths teacher, Mr Barry Wesley, who was also our year advisor had a riotous sense of humour. At this point, he was doubled over, laughing so hard he had to hold his stomach. The soul of generosity, he often gave up his holidays to hold summer study courses for us. He was a very tall man and had a theatrical flair that kept us entertained constantly.

If we couldn't catch on to some complex Maths problem he would throw himself on the floor, tear at his hair, crawl into the foetal position and howl, 'Why me? Why me?'

As the recording kept playing, Mr Solomon appointed himself to quell The Rebellion. He went round all the classrooms and cut the speaker wires with pliers, though later several of the teachers asked where they could acquire a copy of the recording.

After recess, the organised mayhem really began. With the school allowing a reasonable amount of letting off steam, they put rules in place.

No throwing of water or other substances inside. No participation by students other than the school leavers— their turn would come.

Our Maths teacher joined in the fracas. His thick black beard flowed as he yelled, 'Seek and destroy', 'Death to insurgents', 'Floggings at dawn' and other nonsense. He'd brought his own supply of flour, as had our Geography teacher.

By lunchtime, we were all covered in thick white flour crusts that had dried stiff. Bedraggled and tired we went back inside to collect our schoolbags and head off home for the last time.

We found our beloved Mr Wesley had left us a message, written in chalk on the blackboard in his negligent scrawl.

'Veni, vidi, vici—Go forth, conquer the world—and don't come back!' Underneath, in tiny print, was written 'God bless you all.'

A fitting benediction from a marvellous man.

Goodbye lunch with Mum

'You always knew what you wanted,' Mum said. 'I envied that.'

'Really, did you?' I was touched by her sharing with me. We were having our goodbye lunch together before I left for Sydney and nurse's training. Mum had organised just the two of us to eat at our favourite place.

The Oak café at Freeman's Waterhole was on a road that meandered for miles and became the main road through Cooranbong. It was a popular eating place for locals.

'Yes, there weren't many choices for a country girl from Quirindi when there were eight children in the family and a widowed mother.' I waited for her to go on. It was a special moment and Mum's eyes had softened with the thought of our parting and the memories of her own leaving home.

'I didn't want to be a nurse; I could never stomach hospitals or doctors. There was only that or Business College. Anyway I wanted to be a stenographer,' she continued.

'Was that the same as a secretary?' I asked, although I'd heard the explanation many times.

'Well, pretty much I guess. I really wanted to do another year at College, but Mum could only afford one year, even though I worked at the factory for some of my fees. I was a whiz on the comptometer—the adding machine.'

I laughed. 'With your genius at adding I wonder you needed the help of a machine, Mum.' She smiled.

'I was really good at shorthand too, but I didn't have much confidence in those days.' She looked sad. 'I had an inferiority complex when I was young, you know. Found it hard to feel good about myself, especially around people.'

'But you manage a shop.'

'I know, but it's everyday conversation really I find difficult. I never was much good at it. Not like you!' she chuckled.

'But people are so interesting, Mum. I just want to see inside them and find out what makes them tick.'

'You were born like that. Always watching everyone, smiling and gurgling at strangers. You lit up like the sun

A Curious & Inelegant Childhood

when people chatted to you, even before you could talk.'

'I thought you said I was born talking,' I teased.

'Ha, Ha!' she mocked. 'Although that's not far from the truth,' she admitted. 'And whistle! When you weren't talking you whistled. That boarder who lived with Nana Stockdale taught you. I could have killed him!'

'Oh dear, how annoying for you,' I laughed, amazed that we could joke about this. We sat silently for a while, eating our salad sandwiches and watching the ducks on the pond outside.

'Did I always want to be a nurse?' I asked, knowing she never tired of telling this story.

'When you were three years old you told people you were going to be 'a nurse and a typewriter'.'

'Goodness, I wanted to be a machine?'

'Well, you were only three.'

'Maybe I did mean a typewriter. I know I could never be a secretary. Well, not a good one anyway.'

'No. You'd make up the rules as you went along.'

'Somebody has to.'

'Yes, but it's usually the boss!'

'There have to be a few free thinkers in the world, Mum.'

'I'm glad there is one of you.'

I glowed under her praise. We went outside to the market area where there were plants and seedlings for sale. Mum could never resist checking out plants and nurseries, but looking up quickly she saw my attention had wandered.

'Let's go and have an ice-cream,' she said impulsively. Apparently today was my day. As we sat licking our double chocolate ice-creams, we laughed that we couldn't keep up with the melting delight. We chased the drips with our paper serviettes and still ended up with ice-cream on the tabletop.

'You wouldn't think it was fun on your clean table, Mum!'

'I'm sorry for ever hurting you,' she said, out of the blue. So like her—to be suddenly straightforward. 'I haven't always understood you, but you're a good daughter and I'm proud of you.'

'It's okay Mum,' I murmured as unexpected tears pricked my eyes. 'I'm sorry for being headstrong and…'

'Oh stop. You always knew what you wanted, how to get it and never gave up. I wish I'd had half that at your age.'

'I don't think we're meant to understand everything about each other. It's a wonderful journey of discovery.'

'Blooming nuisance if you ask me. Typewriters and adding machines make more sense than people.'

'I love you, Mum.'

'I love you, too.'

She was just another confused traveller in the winding journey of life, this mother of mine. Trying to work it out as she went along and doing her damnedest to keep life on solid ground. She watched me flying into life changing the rules, changing everything.

How frightening it must have been for her, raising this exuberant, ethereal spirit that was her child. She must have tired of life's disasters. Become weary of my crusades. From her world of straight lines and square boxes, I must have looked like an uncontrollable force of nature; unpredictable. Relentless in her pursuit of fairness and a hard day's work, she enjoyed the concrete side of motherhood. She would tick off 'clean, warm, tummies full, tucked up safe in bed', and then she would rest.

She loved me and wanted to pay me the ultimate compliment in life by making me like her, the only way to be in this world that is far from heaven, and full of mystery and questions.

It was time for our goodbye—for even though I was not going far away, I was leaving home. I knew her last words would be the benediction of 'be careful' with all that entails; the unspoken words—'Be safe, come home again back to me, because no matter how angry I am with you or how little I understand you, you are mine and without you in my life, I am undone.'

À bientôt, mes amis

The familiar aroma of creamy, vegetable soup seasoned with bay leaves tantalised my senses. I swung the timber gate wide and ran up the stairs with anticipation. I had come to say good-bye to my teacher and friend, John (Jean) Reynaud, and his wife Paulette. Paulette opened the door, then smiling widely, kissed me on both cheeks.

'John. Come,' she called brightly. 'It is Linda, our Mona Lisa. Come to say good-bye.'

'Ah, Linda,' said John, also kissing me on both cheeks. 'But it is not goodbye, Paulette. It is à bientôt—see you soon. Linda will come to see us often to tell us of her life in the city. Won't you!'

'Oui! À bientôt, mes amis,' I said, laughing.

Little had I thought five years before that I would fall in love with the French language, and come to see my teacher and his family as beloved friends.

The last term in Year 7 meant a widening of subject choices and I was thrilled. There were certain subjects that were obligatory for that one term of Year 7. Then we would choose our permanent subjects at the end of the year for Year 8 and beyond. I wasn't entirely impressed with the idea of 'Domestic Science'. I could see my straight A status slipping from my grasp. Just having the two words 'domestic' and 'science' grouped together was an oxymoron in my opinion. Memories of my 'disasters' at home scalded my thoughts, but when I arrived in the Domestic Science room and smelt the aroma of a gently simmering curry and saw my new teacher, Nelia Rice, with her welcoming smile and graciously folded hands, I knew I had come home.

I continued to love the subject even though my efforts were often rewarded at home with, 'What's this foreign muck?' from my brother, who regarded my new offerings as an insult to his stomach. He may have looked Mediterranean, but his food tastes were strictly British. 'Protein and three veg', followed by anything swimming in custard was his desired fare, which according to me should have stayed in a Charles Dickens novel where it rightly belonged.

In the last term we had to learn French, and I moaned along with the rest of the class. I couldn't even conceive how I'd get my head around another language. But from the moment our new French teacher, Dr John Reynaud, began with the basics I was thoroughly hooked. We were fortunate indeed to have a real Frenchman teach us. Of French parents, John was born in the French colony of Vietnam, in Hanoï. On furlough to Grenoble, in The French Alps, he met and fell in love with his wife Paulette. John Reynaud opened a new world of wonder for me. I now waved away the other kids when they complained about learning French.

'That'd be right, Brooksie! Another bloody subject you love! Are there any you don't like?'

'Course! Maths is boring and Economics is rubbish,' I muttered.

'You're not even doing Economics!'

'Ergo,' I said.

'Oh leave her alone, she's talking French again,' they said scornfully.

'It's not Fr … arrggh.' They'd gone.

When we began studying French in Year 8 it was a small class. This was good news for me. Over the next few years we learnt about French literature, reading 'L'étranger' by Albert Camus. We learned about French cuisine and watched French movies. And all the while I was becoming a part of their family. Somewhere along the way those of us drawn into their circle stepped seamlessly from Mr and Mrs, to John and Paulette. One of their daughters was my age and we became friends. I was a frequent visitor, enjoying this lively family, Paulette's wonderful French cooking and John's constantly curious and intelligent mind.

John fired my imagination and gifted me with the concept that life brought endless possibilities. So many things that were unknown could become a life passion. Wondrous, surprising things could be just around the corner. John shared my thirst for learning and rewarded my endless questions with delight. In many ways he was like my own father, gentle of spirit and always looking to widen his education, always reading. From John I learned the joy of embracing life as a perpetual student. Learning didn't have to end with formal education; there were no limits. My hunger was validated.

Paulette, his wife was grace personified. I loved their home for its welcoming warmth. Paulette began to call me their 'Mona Lisa'. I found this confusing as I couldn't see a resemblance, and secretly thought the woman who inspired the painting as bland and stiff. Perhaps you had to be French, I thought. Curiosity got the better of me and I questioned Paulette.

'Why do you think I'm like the 'Mona Lisa'? The only likeness I see is that we both have black hair. They say she is mysterious and no-one ever has to guess what I'm thinking. I speak my mind too much. And she has a stillness, where I …'

'Ah,' said Paulette. 'You do not see yourself as others do. It is not in the resemblance. And you are wrong, you often have a stillness, but you are alike because there is so much more behind your eyes. There are mysteries you will only share with those who know you well.'

'Oh,' I said, overcome by her words. I did not have the red full-lipped beauty of the women in their opulent fine silks with haughty lustful eyes. I had something else, and for the first time in my life I felt a kind of beauty.

The years flew past and we were soon studying for our final exam. Because there were only two students in the French class, John had lots of time to spend with us individually. 'So Linda, what have you planned for the rest of your life?' asked John smiling, '…apart from learning everything you can.' He smiled. 'You can do anything you set your mind to.' I had been ready to ramble on with my plans, but his words stopped me. In spite of my good grades, this was the first time I had been told I 'could do anything.' I was lost for words. It was in the era when teachers seemed to think that if you were given praise, you would become complacent, unbearably big-headed or stop trying. 'Whatever you choose,' said John, slapping the table with a beaming smile, 'I believe in you. If you tell me that in five years' time you will be here … or there … I believe you. Whatever you set out to do, you will do.'

I had no response and apparently none was needed. I never forgot those words, delivered so clearly and sincerely. At every junction of my life, where decisions beckoned, I remembered that day, and John's words.

We stayed in touch over the years. Now, I often see Paulette or John and revel in the way their eyes light up. In my second year of nurse training John was my patient in Intensive Care. It took a long shower to wash away my burning tears for his health and future.

Farewell to home

Mum gave me one of her old suitcases. After all, I wasn't going far. Even though it was to Sydney, the 'big smoke', it was only two and a half hours away.

I declined the strap that usually held it together. The memory of its sting after childhood punishments was something I wanted to forget. I added my new instamatic camera. Mum fussed and made lists. I chafed at her ministrations and her endless anxious advice. I was an adult now—ready to set sail into life. At least, I was desperately trying to be ready, to gather courage for a brave new world.

'This will always be your home,' she said, patting the purple chenille bedspread in my room that overlooked the backyard.

The backyard of my childhood adventures, where the mulberry tree still held some of the boards, haphazard now, of the tree house we had used as a fort or meeting place.

The mulberry tree still had the rope hanging there, the one we used to slide down to the ground below. I remembered the time I first used it. I had baulked at the descent.

'Go on, Sis! Just slide down as fast as you can!' yelled Peter.

I did, suffering severe rope burns on the way.

'Serves you right, Sis, I didn't mean that fast!' he said.

But he was pained and anxious for me, holding my blistered, burnt hands before running with me to Mum for salve.

I remembered a time, when under that tree, a miracle of life occurred that had deeply offended my mother. Against her better judgment, and dire warnings of catastrophe, Dad had offered to look after the neighbour's pet goat for several weeks while they went on holiday.

Very early the next morning we were awakened to the sound of enough bleating to wake the dead. The goat had given birth to twins in the night.

'That'd be right!' said Mum, with fulminating disgust. 'Now we have three of the blasted things to feed.'

I looked at the long acre paddock where we children had thought it great sport when Dad burnt off the long grass with two hoses at the ready, Peter manning one and Dad the other, while I and any of our friends who were up for fun had stood guard along the fence line with wet hessian bags.

Then, with any accumulated tree branches and left-over timber from Dad's latest project, we had enjoyed a bonfire, sitting close to the crackling flames with our arms wrapped around our knees, watching the sparks spiral heavenward, while the acrid smell of smoke teased our noses. Those were times I would never forget.

I had ruled the world at school and was full of confidence there. I had achieved dux of the school, romped in school plays, and been public speaking since early high school. I was school captain and had received a Commonwealth Scholarship, guaranteeing free university study, but I had turned it down.

Everyone was disappointed, and no-one more so than Mum, for I was 'destined for great things'. But I had seen the vagaries of worldly success and false pride, and decided it was not for me. Even though I was doing the unexpected, the over-achiever accepting 'a lesser life', I was following my heart.

I was going to become the person I chose to be. No one knew how much I wanted to leave my schooldays behind, how little I cared for the kind of success assumed to be my destiny.

I had longed for independence, but I also wanted to start afresh. I wanted to prove myself in a new place, leaving behind the accolades that had come my way. Having little concept of what nursing would be like I wanted desperately to fit in and find my way in life, without the expectations that had followed me through my schooldays.

I wanted to be a nurse, with its ethos of service, its connection to people; its nurturing of the sick and helpless. I would fight for the underdog; change the world, even if just a little. Even if just for a time.

Mum and Dad drove me to my new life, down the old Pacific Highway. We wound the windows down on that slow journey, so we could hear the bellbirds' ringing songs.

And that's where my heart still takes me, when I hear a bellbird sing.

Commies, feminism and ignorance

1973 was a great year to be leaving home and heading off into the world. Australia was withdrawing our troops from Vietnam. This made monumental sense to me even at the ignorant age of 17, not because I was full of political savvy, but because my brother had been drafted. His number had come up. He had been able to defer until he finished his apprenticeship, but then his 'Nasho' service was imminent. Only had a short time when he was saved by the election of Gough Whitlam and the Labor party.

I had been stiff with anxiety about my brother going to war as he appeared to have none of the qualities that would make him of any use in any army. He was shy and gentle and although he enjoyed using the 22 shotgun to shoot aluminium cans off the back fence, I had grave doubts about his enthusiasm or commitment for shooting people. Besides mum could never get him out of bed in the morning, and if *my mother* couldn't get someone up and going there was no Corporal or Sergeant on earth who could.

Don't even mention the option of becoming a medic, because when a complete stranger fell off the back of his friend's motorcycle outside our house and was quite hearty but had his face covered in blood, it wasn't the victim needing to lie down and have a drink of water but my brother. The victim sat calmly in the middle of our lounge room enjoying the attention of all and talking ninety to the dozen.

I experienced an initial period of fear and dread about the election of the Labor party because my mother had expostulated that "the end of the world was around the corner because we now had an atheist Commie government and would soon fall into Godless anarchy, forcing God to intervene Himself." When nothing remotely fatalistic appeared on the world horizon and no-one was even struck by lightning, I calmed down, thinking perhaps she had it wrong and began to relax.

When I overheard my mother calling Gough Whitlam a stupid man because of his quick wit, I developed a great fondness for him as I had also suffered at her hands for 'smart aleck remarks'. Later I went even further and decided that he was obviously a man of superior intelligence when my mother watched him on television, decrying loudly that 'sarcasm is the lowest form of wit'. She was fond of conversing with the television, perhaps with the vain hope that the person she was addressing would hear her and wither into silence. This character denunciation had often been thrown at both my father and I, so Gough's position in our affection was assured.

Equality had arrived for women. The government had just given women equal pay. I was thrilled to find out about feminism and the new freedoms for women until I discovered that it bore little difference to my mother's own philosophy of 'no man is going to damn well tell me what to do, or when to do it'. She had worked as long as I could remember as manager of the corner grocery store.

She constantly expressed amazement at the women of her acquaintance who gave up all vestiges of independence, allowed men to 'rule the roost', went without cars and driver's licenses and generally would usually take "a blind bit of notice of anything just because it came from a man."

Her pithy 'what would they know', had more effect on me than the most compelling lecture on Modern Feminism. As my father was relied upon and greatly respected by her in all matters where he was superior, I wondered what all the fuss was about. Equality of the sexes had been effectively functioning in our house as long as I could remember.

I can remember a social gathering of some of my aunts and several other women from our church. One elegant Stepford wannabee folded her daintily gloved hands and declared, "I rely on my husband for everything, I don't even know how to use the washing machine."

My mother was thoroughly stunned by this remark and regarded the woman with a look that she normally reserved for the criminally insane.

"How's that going to work for you after he's dead, Elaine?" said my mother, who would never be sent on a diplomatic mission to any country, other than one where war was considered necessary and immediate.

A tense silence filled the room. The woman blanched at the introduction of such remarks over afternoon tea and clattered her cup to the saucer, suddenly finding something of interest to focus on out of the window.

'They do you know, die I mean," added my mother emphatically, never knowing when to leave well enough alone. "Might as well face facts." My mother felt that it was her Christian duty to prepare this woman for reality, but the poor soul gave every appearance of being scarred for life.

Acknowledgements

I would like to thank my sons for their patience, tolerance and love, and for never criticising my writing, because they couldn't be bothered to read any of it.

I am indebted to my friends for their unconditional acceptance and for laughing and crying with me, sometimes at the same time. I am blessed to have the friendship of Cathy and John Duffy, the editors of the Cooranbong Gazette, who gave their support, creative input and publish many of my stories.

To my mother, who gave me a warm bed, a full belly, a roof over my head, an education, and a floor clean enough that I could have eaten off it had I so desired. To my father, for the priceless treasure of unconditional love, wit, grace and endless patience. For sharing his love of music with me, and for living his creed and faith.

To my father's sister, my Auntie Gwen who said, 'I don't want treasures. I want you. You're my treasure.' And to all the other aunties who adopted me.

To my brother Peter, for not dying when I punched him in the nose, and for not electrocuting me, although he tried. To my paternal grandmother for creating a love of stories when I sat at her feet as a child. To my maternal grandmother for listening to my awkward attempts to play 'Amazing Grace' and for giving me "two bob" to buy ice-creams saying, 'Don't tell your mother.'

Special thanks go to Pina and Martin of Universal Micro for answering questions that made no sense to anyone else.

Special thanks are reserved for Margaret at the Cooranbong Newsagency for staff with heart. It's my lucky place, even though I still haven't won the lottery.

www.ingramcontent.com/pod-product-compliance
Lightning Source LLC
Chambersburg PA
CBHW071231070526
44583CB00017B/2133